PRAISE FOR *WALKING IN LIGHT*

"In her wonderful new book, Sandra Ingerman, one of the great shamanic teachers of our time, offers us ways to become shamans of our own souls and healers of our own lives. She incites us to come to our senses in the animated, spirited universe. Open this book on almost any page, and you will find a door to the Otherworld. *Walking in Light* stirs us to wake up inside the dream of this life, and change the dream if it does not suit our soul's purpose. This book is highly recommended for both neophytes and advanced practitioners. It calls us to make and live our own creation stories and walk in tenderness and joy on this good earth as stars who came down because we wanted a juicier life."

ROBERT MOSS
author of *Conscious Dreaming, Dreaming the Soul Back Home,* and *The Boy Who Died and Came Back*

"It's your birthright to live an inspired and purposeful life—illuminated by the radiance of your soul. In these pages, Sandra Ingerman lovingly guides you into the profound, ongoing ceremony that is shamanic living. Allow her to inspire you to transform the mundane into the sacred and open your heart to the enduring beauty that unites all that is. The journey to awaken the marvelous change-maker you were born to be starts now!"

EVELYN C. RYSDYK
author of *Spirit Walking: A Course in Shamanic Power*
and *A Spirit Walker's Guide to Shamanic Tools*

"The practices, journeys, and insights in *Walking in Light* offer a step-by-step guide that will help you refine your soul's journey, deepen your relationship with spirit and nature, and consciously participate with the creative force of life. Sandra shares brilliantly, in a down-to-earth and detailed manner, how we can nurture our heartfelt longings and support positive planetary change during these evolving times. This is a master guidebook!"

LLYN ROBERTS, MA
award-winning author of *Shapeshifting into Higher Consciousness*
and *Shamanic Reiki* (with Robert Levy)

"In *Walking in Light,* Sandra Ingerman, calling herself a spiritual explorer, leads us to explore our own inner worlds to seek our spiritual identities. From her own life experiences and shamanic practice, she tells us she has 'fine-tuned' her work and teaching as she continues to share the solid advice and instruction that her students have come to expect. Her message to all of us, whether seasoned shamanic practitioners or newcomers, is to fine-tune our own spiritual paths, to not put our shamanic practice 'in a box,' but to experiment in order to keep it alive, relevant, and vital."

TOM COWAN
author of *Fire in the Head, Shamanism as a Spiritual Practice for Daily Life,* and *Yearning for the Wind*

"Once again Sandra Ingerman has written a superb, highly practical, and comprehensive book about practicing the shamanic way of life—and the best part of all, with simplicity and kindness. Here Sandra demonstrates the wisdom gained from many years of dedicated hard work walking her own sometimes very challenging shamanic path. What I most appreciated is that throughout the book she takes a non-rigid, flexible approach, emphasizing creativity and living from the heart. It is as if she is taking you by the hand and guiding you personally through each step and consideration in the process. If there were ever an excellent basic manual to shamanic practice, this would be it."

JOSÉ LUIS STEVENS, PHD
author of *Awaken the Inner Shaman, The Power Path,* and *Secrets of Shamanism*

"*Walking in Light* by Sandra Ingerman is more than just a deeper understanding of the work of a shaman. It's an everyday guide to help you tap into your inner wisdom, integrate the shamanic practices, and activate the power of love within. This book will not only help beginners of the shamanic way but also people who have been working with these practices for a while."

GARY QUINN
intuitive life coach and bestselling author of
May the Angels Be With You and *The Yes Frequency*

"Sandra Ingerman is a modern medicine woman whose book *Walking in Light* has brought together more than 30 years of her teaching and practice in an ancient yet curiously immediate spiritual tradition called shamanism. Among the indigenous peoples, it was always understood that each new generation had the responsibility to perpetuate and refresh a continuously recreated body of wisdom and technique, even adding to and changing the accumulating treasure of the shamanic tradition across time . . . for it was always in this way that it remained vital and meaningful to those who walked the shaman's path. Sandra Ingerman has done just this, and she is to be commended for creating very good medicine indeed. I love this book!"

HANK WESSELMAN, PHD
anthropologist and author of eight books on shamanism including
The Bowl of Light, the award-winning *Awakening to the Spirit World*
(with Sandra Ingerman), and the *Spiritwalker* trilogy

"Awaken with Sandra Ingerman's new book and walk into the light of your destiny. Sandra will take you by the hand and help reveal your inner self in order to find and achieve your true call and vision for the future. See how following the shamanic life leads you to a sense of inner peace, and triggers the creation of your mind to put into action all of these deep thoughts buried within. We all need to become Peace in Action in order to complete the sentence 'I think, therefore I am' with 'therefore I do!' It's in the doing that our being finds the true meaning of its existence. *Walking in Light* will indeed empower you and reveal the path to your inner and outer world."

EMMANUEL ITIER
director/producer of the award-winning documentary
Femme and CEO of Wonderland Entertainment

WALKING IN
LIGHT

Also by Sandra Ingerman

BOOKS

Soul Retrieval: Mending the Fragmented Self

Welcome Home: Following Your Soul's Journey Home

A Fall to Grace (fiction)

*Medicine for the Earth: How to Transform Personal
and Environmental Toxins*

Shamanic Journeying: A Beginner's Guide (book and drumming CD)

How to Heal Toxic Thoughts: Simple Tools for Personal Transformation

Awakening to the Spirit World: The Shamanic Path of Direct Revelation,
co-authored by Hank Wesselman (book and drumming CD)

*The Shaman's Toolkit: Ancient Tools for Shaping the Life
and World You Want to Live In*

Speaking with Nature: Awakening to the Deep Wisdom of the Earth,
co-authored by Llyn Roberts

AUDIO PROGRAMS

The Soul Retrieval Journey

Miracles for the Earth

The Beginner's Guide to Shamanic Journeying

Shamanic Meditations: Guided Journeys for Insight, Vision, and Healing

Soul Journeys: Music for Shamanic Practice

*Shamanic Visioning: Connecting with Spirit to Transform
Your Inner and Outer Worlds* (6-CD audio program)

Shamanic Visioning Music: Taiko Drum Journeys

WALKING IN LIGHT

---

the Everyday
Empowerment
of a Shamanic Life

SANDRA INGERMAN

sounds true
BOULDER, COLORADO

Sounds True
Boulder, CO 80306

This work is solely for personal growth and education. It should not be
treated as a substitute for professional assistance, therapeutic activities such
as psychotherapy or counseling, or medical advice. In the event of physical
or mental distress, please consult with appropriate health professionals.
The application of protocols and information in this book is the choice of
each reader, who assumes full responsibility for his or her understandings,
interpretations, and results. The author and publisher assume no
responsibility for the actions or choices of any reader.

Published 2014
Cover design by Jennifer Miles
Book design by Beth Skelley

FSC
www.fsc.org
MIX
From responsible
sources
FSC® C103098

Printed in the United States of America

Library of Congress Cataloging-in-Publication Data
Ingerman, Sandra.
  Walking in light : the everyday empowerment of a shamanic life /
Sandra Ingerman.
    pages cm
Includes bibliographical references and index.
ISBN 978-1-62203-428-4
1. Spiritual life. 2. Shamanism. 3. Light—Religious aspects. I. Title.
BF1999.I549 2014
201'.44—dc23

                              2014027469

Ebook ISBN 978-1-62203-452-9

10 9 8 7

To my helping spirits who light my way
and to the Earth, which is my home.
In honor of my parents, Aaron and Lee Ingerman,
and to my husband, Woods.

Contents

Preface

Although I felt support from my family and teachers when I was growing up, I felt like I never received an "operating manual" for how to live in the ordinary world. I had a good childhood. I had loving parents, and although my brother and I fought a lot, we had a great relationship. I loved going to school and learning new things. Even as a child I had a deep spiritual life and was comfortable in the spiritual realms. But while I had spiritual experiences, I had no path to follow.

This was the 1960s, a very wild time as people my age were looking to birth a new consciousness into the world. I searched for ways to feel connected with life, but found myself floundering and at a loss for how to live a meaningful life. As a teenager I was involved in protesting the Vietnam War. I felt so disempowered as I felt so strongly that the war was unjust. No matter how I felt, I had no power to create change.

That is why when I was introduced to the practice of shamanic journeying in 1980, I received a great gift. I met my helping spirit, a guardian spirit who over the years answered my questions about how to bring joy, meaning, and health into my life. Shamanism provided me with a path and structure to follow to deepen my spiritual path. I found the empowerment I needed by engaging in the practice of shamanism as a way of life.

As I continued to work with my guardian spirit and a variety of other helping spirits, I learned that the practice of shamanism is more than just performing journeys into the invisible realms to access information. Shamanism is a way of life. So I started teaching shamanism as a way to change our lives and the world around us.

As a part of this work, which I call Medicine for the Earth, I was invited by the School of Integrative Medicine at the University of Michigan to participate in a pilot research study to explore the effects of Medicine for the Earth on people who had suffered a heart attack. In the study there were three groups. One group worked with me and learned shamanic principles that I teach in Medicine for the Earth. This group was compared to a group that received standard cardiac care and another group that participated in a life-change retreat run by the University of Michigan Cardiovascular Center focusing on nutrition, physical exercise, and stress management.[1]

The study used a variety of standard physical and mental benchmarks to track the success of the program. The Medicine for the Earth group had an immediate 50 percent reduction on their depression score using the Beck Depression Inventory. The Medicine for the Earth group also showed a marked improvement on a test measuring hope. This improvement with their depression and levels of hope remained six months later.

This was a randomized study, and I had no control over who participated in my group. The majority of the group members were conservative Christians. The people in the group were extraordinary and all a joy to work with, and I learned from working with these wonderful people that I could teach shamanic principles that created healing and a state of hope to people of all religious faiths. The conclusion of the published pilot research study was that a spiritual retreat such as Medicine for the Earth could be used to increase hope while reducing depression in persons with acute coronary depression.[2]

In today's world, being able to maintain a state of hope is critical to staying emotionally and physically healthy. When we move into prolonged states of despair, we are drained of the vitality we need to imagine the creative solutions needed to shift our life in a new direction, which will ultimately help us evolve and live a deeper and more meaningful life. As long as we have hope, we have a foundation upon which positive change and healing can occur.

My own life story is a journey of healing from severe depression. I chose to follow a spiritual path for my healing. On some deep level I understood that my depression was an initiation into shamanism and the path of the wounded healer. Every practice I share in *Walking in Light* has been woven into my daily life. These practices have truly been my "healing balm." I have learned through my journeys and the spiritual practices that I share how to ride the waves of depression, which has led me to a rich, deep, and meaningful life.

As I stay in touch with participants from the courses I teach all over the world, as well as the readers of my monthly column, it is clear that those who continue to apply what I teach and practice a shamanic way of life reap great benefits. But this work is not always easy to follow. As my own path has revealed, it does require a great deal of discipline and persistence. Sometimes it just feels easier to fall back into a way of life that does not call us to stay focused on our behavior throughout the day. This work asks us to make a firm choice to be diligent with the practices.

I am excited to share with you what I have learned over my years of teaching how to incorporate shamanic practices into everyday life and hence be in service to all life on the planet. For all of life is connected; every shift in consciousness that you are empowered to make each and every moment ripples throughout the entire web of life.

Introduction

ALTHOUGH SHAMANISM IS AN ANCIENT PRACTICE, it is relevant to all of us today who are seeking ways to live a life filled with harmony, good health, and returning balance and peace back to our lives and to the planet. As a licensed psychotherapist, my passion in teaching shamanism has been how to bridge such an ancient way of working into the Western world to deal with the current challenges that we face. Shamanism is a practice that continues to evolve to meet the needs of the times and the cultural needs of the people. The ability of the practice of shamanism to evolve is why it continues to be so relevant today: thousands of people are embracing unity consciousness and the use of light and sound for healing. I feel strongly that shamanic practitioners must continue to evolve their work in order to stay current and keep the practice of shamanism relevant to today's world.

In this regard *Walking in Light* is not just a beginning course on shamanic journeying. Rather, this book will take you into your inner realms, where you will learn how to live a shamanic way of life that embraces a state of joy that bubbles up from a deep place within. You will learn how to center yourself in the midst of change and be able to stay focused and filled with hope no matter what is going on in the outer world. You will acquire tools to help you wake up each day being present to what life brings to and for you, for life always brings us situations and experiences to help us grow, deepen who we are, and evolve. We need to learn how to change our perception to see how life's challenges are all part of the life adventure we signed up for.

You will experience more confidence about how to better flow through the river of life, not just the smooth waters but also through turbulent ones. It is important to recognize that life is filled with cycles that change. And it is important to learn how to cooperate with change rather than resisting or fighting changes that occur in our lives.

In *Walking in Light,* I share a variety of practices that will help to better cultivate your inner life, which leads to a better outer world. You need to regain a state of health and well-being within, as everything that you experience within is reflected back to you in the outer world. As you learn how to be peaceful, balanced, joyful, and grateful, the world will reflect back that state to you. The ultimate goal is to create a healthy inner landscape. You will grow from within. Before we can fully express ourselves in the world, we need to grow from the inside out. When you cultivate a rich inner landscape, you step into a new, beautiful dimension of life.

When people travel to learn from shamans in indigenous cultures, one of the qualities they are struck by is how shamans exude and radiate a light that uplifts everybody who comes into their presence. It's their presence that heals, not so much the methods they perform or what they do. It is the energy behind the method that heals. In our culture we tend to be "addicted" to methods, forgetting that ultimately being a vessel of love is the greatest form of healing.

Shamans laugh a lot. Their eyes sparkle with joy, and they carry an inner peace that most of us in the Western world wish we could feel. Shamans have great compassion for suffering, which comes from being a "wounded healer." Their personal initiatory experiences take them to a place of feeling deep suffering in life so that they will always maintain a state of compassion. The scars and memories of their wounds sculpt away the ego, allowing the depth of their spiritual light to shine forth. They attain a state of inner peace by developing a rich inner world. Many people in our culture only focus on making changes in the outer world. Well, of course we need to come up with plans for our life, but we need to balance out our rational planning with exploring our inner world and learning how to cultivate a rich, peaceful, and powerful inner space. We need to move from outer visioning to the power of working with our inner visions. We need to wake up out of the collective trance that teaches us to only focus on the material realm. It is time to explore how to open ourselves to new dimensions of life.

Once we learn how to do this, our inner wisdom and spirit informs us in ways that are beyond our rational thinking. In *Walking in Light,* I teach you how to travel into the world of the shaman. This world has many aspects. Besides cultivating a rich inner landscape, the shaman also works with helping guardian spirits and allies who can provide wisdom, guidance, and healing.

Shamans live a life of honor and respect for nature. Inherent in sha-manic teachings is the understanding that we are part of nature rather than being separate from it. We learn how to live and flow with the river of life, instead of flowing against it. In shamanic cultures people honor themselves, each other, and all in the web of life leading to a harmonious way of life. The Earth is our home. The only way for life to be sustained is by reconnecting with nature.

Many of us only perceive the world with our ordinary eyes. We walk the path of ego guided by our thoughts, beliefs, fears, and social conditioning. This way of living can lead us to feeling empty. Our soul yearns to touch spirit and to live a meaningful life. When we walk the path of spirit, we perceive our lives and the world from a place of peace, love, and confidence. It takes a great deal of personal work to shift from walking the path of ego to one of spirit. *Walking in Light* provides you with tools to cross the bridge. I invite you to cross the bridge with me and others in the global community.

THE SHAMAN IN HISTORY

In this book, I will lead you in shamanic practices that you can bridge into your day-to-day life. It is important to understand I will not be teaching you how to become a shaman. The spirits choose a person who is to be initiated into the path of becoming a shaman for his or her com-munity. It is not a profession you choose, rather it is part of one's destiny.

Shamanism is an ancient universal spiritual practice that dates back over a hundred thousand years. The word *shaman* comes from the Tungus tribe in Siberia and means "spiritual healer" or "one who sees in the dark." Shamanism has been practiced in Siberia, Asia, Europe,

Africa, Australia, Greenland, and North and South America. As shamanism has been practiced all over the world, you most likely have personal ancestors who at one time practiced shamanism.

A shaman is a man or a woman who uses the ability to see with his or her strong eye. Shamanism is a path of opening the heart, creating a doorway that leads us to traveling into hidden realms. In the hidden realms, the shaman interacts directly with helping, compassionate spirits to divine information and to ask for healing help on behalf of a client or the community. In the practice of shamanism, the spiritual aspect of illness is addressed. An illness might manifest on an emotional or physical level. But in working with shamanic healing, the shaman is shown the spiritual aspect of the illness. There are some general diagnoses of illness, but there are a wide variety of ceremonies that a shaman might perform on behalf of the client. The key to successful shamanic healing is for the shaman to open up and become a vessel of the unlimited power of the helping spirits. It is important to design an individualized treatment plan for each client in need of healing.

The main diagnoses of illness include soul loss, where a client might have lost a part of his soul due to experiencing a trauma. Also a client might have lost some of her power, or there might be a spiritual blockage that needs to be removed. A client could also be dealing with a possessing spirit who has taken up residence in his body. In most cases there are a combination of these issues occurring. The shaman works in partnership with his or her helping spirits to diagnose the problem. The shaman works on behalf of the community to retrieve lost soul parts, to retrieve lost power, and to extract and remove spiritual blockages that don't belong in the body.[1]

Shamans also perform ceremonies to lead souls of the deceased to the transcendent realms. This includes performing psychopomp work to help a client suffering from a possessing spirit. The role of the shaman is also to divine information for a client or for the community. Shamans are not simply technicians of healing and divination methods. They have always acted and still act as healers, doctors, priest and priestesses, psychotherapists, mystics, and storytellers.

Besides performing ceremonies for healing, there are a variety of other ceremonies that shamans perform. Shamans lead ceremonies to welcome children into the world, perform marriages, help people transition to a good place at the time of death, and mourn the death of loved ones. There are important initiation ceremonies performed to mark transitions in a person's life, such as moving from childhood to adulthood.

In a traditional culture there was one or more shamans who performed healing for the community. At the same time, from childhood, everyone was taught ways to live a life of honor, respect, and harmony with oneself, the community, and nature. It was the responsibility of every person who lived in the community to share his or her creative talents and to live in harmony with each other and with nature. Each member of the community was taught from a young age what gifts they share and how vital each person was to the entire community. Each person knew their unique "medicine" they contributed to the health of the community. In Native American cultures *medicine* refers to sacred gifts.

SHAMANISM TODAY

In our culture we are taught how to fit in with society. It is time for us to look at how each of us is also responsible for living a life of honor and respect for all of life and the Earth. Each of us has valuable strengths that contribute to the health of the web of life. In this way we begin to move from a hierarchical model to what I view as a feminine model of honoring our inner wisdom and intuition and working from a place of cooperation and collaboration to be in service to all of life.

The practice of shamanism teaches us that everything that exists is alive and has a spirit. Shamanic cultures recognize that there is a web of life that connects all that is alive. Everything that is alive is called *the spirit that lives in all things.* Everything on Earth is interconnected. Any belief that we are separate from other life forms or living beings—such as the Earth, the stars, the wind—is purely an illusion, and it's the shaman's role in the community to keep harmony and balance between humankind and the forces of nature.

I use the metaphor that we are all part of a giant symphony of life. We each have a note or tone that combines with the notes and tones of the rest of life to create a universal song. We all have something to add to the music and to the song of the universe. It is time to honor our own song.

Shamanism is a practice of direct revelation. And all that you need to learn can be obtained by working with helping spirits as well as tapping into your inner wisdom and vision. We all have creative gifts that we contribute to the collective. We all have the ability to be a presence of love and light that transforms our life, thereby changing the world.

Many of our ancestors experienced religious and political persecution and were imprisoned or even killed if they performed shamanic work. Due to missionary influence, the practice of shamanism was outlawed, as the principle of direct revelation was not supported. And in some countries, such as in Central Asia, governments did not support spiritual practices such as shamanism. Any practice that might question authority was oppressed. Shamans were imprisoned if they were caught drumming or performing ceremony. But I consider it to be our birthright to practice direct revelation and to be in contact with our personal spiritual guidance. Today, we might not practice the same way as people do in native cultures, and it is vital to bridge the ancient ways so that we can work within our culture. As long as we use discipline and stay focused on our spiritual path, we do not take away from the power of the work.

While you might not have been born with the destiny to be a shaman, it is your responsibility to live a spiritual way of life. The practices in *Walking in Light* teach you how to do this.

COMPLEX ISSUES CAN CALL
FOR SIMPLE PRACTICES

Through social media, mail, and e-mail, I am in touch with a large population of people searching for both ways to improve their own life and also ways to be in service to the planet. I continue to write about the power of shamanic practices to create positive change. And I am continuously asked by people where to even start with the spiritual work. I refer people to the practices shared in *Walking in Light.*

At first glance when reading over some of the practices, they look so simple. Some people conclude that what looks simple are practices for beginners. Many of us equate complex practices with advanced work. This is a misperception. In the spiritual community there are perpetual seekers who keep looking for complex ceremonies and practices that on the outside look like they might be more powerful. Many people studying spiritual traditions don't stick with the practices long enough and don't have persistence to reap the rewards. Once you find that path you have been searching for, it is important to stay true to the path, sink into the work, and not get distracted by other ways that look more powerful on the outside. All spiritual paths, however simple in appearance, lead to the same ultimate outcome. The key is doing the work. Many of us love to engage in shamanic healing ceremonies, and we experience a state of ecstasy in doing so. But unless we engage in the everyday empowerment of a shamanic way of life, the healing ceremonies we perform don't have a true lasting effect.

Simple practices that are passed down through shamanic cultures are potent ways to create great transformation. So don't be tricked by how simple these practices are. For they are multilayered, and as you proceed with the work presented in *Walking in Light,* you will find yourself on an adventure where the path is full of joy and is easy and beautiful to walk on.

Then obstacles are put in your path. These obstacles can be complex and might come from unworked material in your unconscious that reveals itself to be looked at, explored, and healed. The collective energies of loved ones, family, friends, and co-workers might not support your living a conscious way of life. You might find that the dynamics of your relationships pull you off your path, leading you to question the work. The same might be true as you continue to engage with the collective societal, cultural, or political energies of the planet that support giving up on dreams, staying in a trance state, and asking you to follow the norm.

I have stayed in touch with so many students who continue to work with this material, and they share with me the benefits they have reaped from both the work and also the challenges presented by living a shamanic life every day. Once they dive in and start the work, they find themselves swimming in complex layers and deep into their personal landscape where they discover great beauty and also some old painful wounds that need to be healed.

HOW TO WORK WITH THE PRACTICES

On this path, you will learn a great deal about yourself. To gain access to the well of knowledge that exists within, you will learn to use the practice of shamanic journeying. While there are many ways for you to tap into that guidance—the inner place of wisdom, intuition, and grace that lives inside of you—what I found in my own life is that shamanic journeying is a wonderful beginning to learn how to access your own information and gain insights about yourself. And then, as you access this information by meeting and working with helping spirits, you can learn how to integrate these practices into to your moment-to-moment life, whether you are standing in line at the bank, waiting to pump gas at the gas station, or driving in traffic. Weaving the invisible into your daily life is the focus of this book. You will feel empowered by doing so.

If you already know the art of shamanic journeying, please review the instructions I give. As I continue to teach and reflect on the practice of shamanism, I fine-tune my instructions. You might pick up new ideas and be inspired to make some changes to your practice that will increase your level of mastery with the work.

We often try to follow instructions of how to perform our spiritual work and forget that the instructions help us get to the door. To go through the doorway and into the true depth of the unseen, we need to let go of the instructions and the methods. The "instructions" can keep us on the surface and limit us from a true exploration of the beauty of the world of spirit. We all have to start somewhere, so the instructions I share will help get you started. However at some point it will be time to let go of the instructions and find your own way. Shamans work with the invisible worlds and formless energies. When we impose too much form on the work, we end up limiting the power.

Because you might find a doorway into the invisible realms that works for you that might not work for others, I present many ways for you to work. Please do not put your shamanic practice "in a box." Experiment with different ways of working and follow your intuition.

Take your time with the material that I share with you. Work in a way so that your psyche can integrate the material before moving onto a new chapter. If you only read this book without performing the exercises, you will only feed your mind. To experience true change, you need to engage in the work. The teachings are beyond the words written. Work slowly and allow your soul to be nurtured by the practices you engage in. As you continue with the practices in the book, start to integrate them into your daily life.

For those of you new to the work, please feel free to skip any journeys you do not feel ready for. You can come back to them at another time when you feel that the time is right for you. There is no proper order to follow. *Walking in Light* is a guide to how to live a shamanic way of life. You want to integrate the practices in the book into your daily life in a slow, steady rhythm.

And for those of you who *have* had the opportunity to work with some of the material presented in this book, take the opportunity to repeat exercises to access a deeper level. Every practice presented in *Walking in Light* has many levels to it. Shamans repeat and live these practices for a lifetime. The practices are not just to be worked with one time only; shamanism is a life path.

Now it is time for you to explore the world of the shaman. It has been so inspiring to watch as my students and peers join me in sharing this work in their communities all over the world. You are joining together with others in creating a collective field of energy and performing this work together. Shamanism is a practice that is outside of time. Therefore, although other readers are doing the practices at different times than you, there is still an exponential power created with the work. As you begin *Walking in Light,* you step into a collective ceremony. The ceremony begins now.

1

BEING a SHAMAN

I INVITE YOU TO GET COMFORTABLE. Start by taking a few deep, cleansing breaths. Notice how breathing deeply leads you to feeling more grounded and centered. As you continue to take some deep breaths imagine these breaths dissolving your distracting thoughts, thoughts of the day, events in your life that might be weighing on you. Imagine moving your energy from your head down into your heart. Put your hands on your heart and breathe. Take a deep breath in, pause. Exhale slowly. Repeat this and connect with your heartbeat. As you do this, feel your connection with the Earth. Experience your connection with your Self—who you are beyond your skin and your mind. Connect with your Self that is a source of stability and permanence, balance and peace. Feel your connection with your Self and the Earth, and the Spirit of the Land where you live.

Shamans perceive everything that exists as alive and as having a spirit. The land where you live is alive too. Connect your heartbeat with the heartbeat of the Earth. Shamanism is a path of the heart, and in this section I will be speaking to your heart, not to your mind.

Now, as you relax and connect with your inner world, feel what you love about life, the preciousness of life. When we really love life and feel passion and meaning for life, that love will always light our way. Love and passion for life always acts as a beacon lighting the way through any challenge you might experience. Feel your love of life by reflecting on something that is precious to you. This might be something in nature; it might be a child you love, a family member, a favorite animal, or a favorite flower. Place the image, the feeling, the sound, or the fragrance of what you love into your heart and breathe deeply, connecting with yourself and the Earth.

Take a few deep breaths and bring your awareness back into the room. You are now ready to learn about helping spirits and the art of shamanic journeying. There is a variety of helping spirits who will share their guidance and support as you step forth on the path of living a shamanic life.

1

Ceremony *and* Doorways *to* Access *the* Hidden Realms

PERFORMING CEREMONIES IS AN IMPORTANT part of life in shamanic communities. Ceremonies are a way for people living in community to support each individual and the collective. It is a way for us as humans to connect with the spiritual world and create a relationship and interaction between the visible and invisible realms. Oftentimes people in Western cultures fear performing ceremonies as we are not taught about the power and how and why they are created. Ceremony remains mysterious to us, and we often fear what we do not understand. For some people, ceremony is too associated with religion, and they might reject having to engage in that form of work, which has no personal meaning for them.

That said, ceremonies have been used in shamanic cultures since the beginning of time. They have been seen as a powerful agent of change and a way for communities to gather together. Through ceremony we set an intention into motion. This opens up a door into the invisible realms where the "as within" meets the "as without," creating a resonant energy that leads to change. Ceremony creates a relationship between humans and the creative forces of the universe where intention leads to an action that manifests as change in the physical world. Through ceremony the shaman divines information and performs healing on behalf of individuals in need. Ceremony is also used to honor important rites and passages and transitions in life, to call in a desired outcome, and to release energies and states of consciousness that no longer serve the individuals and the community at large.

Throughout *Walking in Light* you will learn how to perform divination and healing ceremonies for yourself. You will learn how to create ceremonies where you are not following rules and instructions, rather you will be creating ceremonies that have personal meaning for you. You will also explore how to enrich your spiritual life by living each day as a ceremony. In this way you weave the sacred into your ordinary reality. Sometimes people engage in spiritual practices believing that by doing so they will be protected from the challenges of life. But please remember that life brings you situations to help you grow and evolve. Neither ceremony nor helping spirits will protect you from the challenges of life. Spiritual practices give you the tools to deal with what life brings for you. The challenges start to wear your ego and mind down, and your body gets tired. This allows your spirit to shine through, lighting the way. Your inner spirit has the strength to carry you through. The key is strengthening your connection with your inner spirit.

Shamanic work moves you from operating from the small *will*. This is the egoic will where you try to force movement in your life. Surrender opens you to the big *WILL*. This is your inner spirit—divine self. Once you surrender to *WILL*, you find yourself living a spiritually driven life. This leads to experiencing your inner shaman, for you cannot operate out of fear and live from a place of spirit at the same time.

Part of doing your personal work is learning how to live from your heart and be guided through life by your heart and your strong eye—where you have access to your intuition. You cannot sleep through the challenges life presents you with. And you cannot power through with the strength of only your body and mind. The strength of your spirit will carry you through.

Many of us wonder if life is going to get easier for us. It depends on what you choose—following the stream of ego or choosing spirit. You must develop a strong connection with your divine light, source, and inner spirit. Once you do that, you will then be able to surrender to the strength of your spirit. You will feel like you are truly being carried by spirit through life. You will feel more graceful as you ride the river of life. As you learn through experience to trust your inner spirit and inner guidance along with the support from your helping spirits, the more you will feel empowered in your daily life and experience the inner transformation that will be reflected back to you in the outer world.

A core principle in spiritual teachings is that our outer world is a reflection of our inner state of consciousness. The esoteric teaching "as above, so below; as within, so without" is also a shamanic understanding. Changing your inner landscape through ceremony transforms you, and your outer world will reflect those changes back to you. You will feel empowered in your daily life. You begin to be guided by spirit instead of just following your ego. You start to ride a different wave of life than you have been riding before, and you begin to feel harmonious and peaceful inside. This creates healing for yourself and also in the world, for harmony within always creates harmony without. Each "ceremony," each change in consciousness you make, ripples throughout the entire web of life.

CREATING CEREMONY

When you set aside the time and put in the physical effort to perform a ceremony indoors or in nature, you will notice a potency to the work. In performing a ceremony your body gets engaged. Your mind has to design the ceremony. You need to collect supplies and find the right place to perform the ceremony and set up sacred space. Your inner spirit is present, carrying you through and supporting you. There is a focus created in performing a ceremony where body, mind, and spirit join together and engage with concentration and focus to create a desired outcome. Ceremonies have a beginning, a middle, and an end.

BEGINNING

The beginning is designing the ceremony, collecting the tools you need, and creating sacred space. You have to prepare yourself so that you are entering into the Dreamtime as you perform your ceremony. Setting a strong intention for your ceremony is key to creating a positive outcome.

There might be something special you want to wear such as sacred clothes, a scarf, belt, or special jewelry. This is a way of stepping out of your ordinary life and entering into the world of spirit. When shamans wear their costumes during ceremonies, it is a way to move from an egoic state into being one with the power of spirit. Here are some other ways to prepare:

Take some time to be in silence reflecting on your intention.

Sing and dance to move your ego aside and let the power of spirit shine through you.

You can drum and rattle to shift out of an ordinary state of consciousness.

You can place sacred objects at your ceremonial site to support your work.

Use your imagination. This is a time to call in and welcome your helping spirits and all the spiritual allies who you wish to honor for their presence in witnessing your work. Welcoming the helping spirits is a way to be courteous as you invite them to be partners with you in your work. When I lead ceremonies, I use some variation of the guided meditation to welcome and honor the helping spirits that I will share with you in chapter 2. You are welcome to use this example in your own ceremony and to adapt it as seems appropriate to you and your intention.

MIDDLE

Performing the actual ceremony is the middle. You can design a simple ceremony, or you can create a more elaborate one. Through experience you might notice that performing a simple ceremony feeds your soul. Performing an elaborate ceremony can keep you tied to your mind. There isn't a right or wrong way to perform a ceremony. Ceremony is an action done with intention. The inherent power of ceremony is to act out your strong intention by concentrating on your intention while performing actions and holding a very strong focus. You do not want to make your ceremony so complex that you end up losing your concentration and focus.

Some people read a letter or poem they have written to the spirits. There are those who burn a piece of paper, an act that states an intention they wish to release into the universe. Others drum and sing as they focus on a desire they wish to manifest. In this book, you will find suggestions for activities you can perform during ceremonies for different purposes.

I find that many people are afraid of performing ceremonies as they fear they might do something wrong. The keys to performing a successful ceremony are calling in your helping spirits through intention and holding your intention of what you wish the outcome of your ceremony to be.

ENDING

The end is a time of closure and stating that the work is done. When you feel complete, let the helping spirits know that your work is done for now. This is a way to honor the helping spirits who have been working in partnership with you. It is simply a matter of courtesy to thank them and say that the work done. This is accomplished by thanking the elements and all the spiritual forces that held you in love and witnessed your transformation and healing. You can leave sacred offerings in gratitude to all the spiritual allies who worked with you in partnership. Returning to an ordinary state of consciousness helps you to fully end the ceremony while feeling grounded at the same time.

When you end your ceremony, don't judge or overanalyze how you performed the ceremony. Once you set your intention in the beginning, the helping spirits in the invisible realms work with you in partnership to manifest that intention. Once you close your ceremony, reflect on the beauty of the work you have done. In indigenous cultures, people in the community always end by saying how beautiful a ceremony was.

When you engage in a ceremony that you perform regularly, you must stay diligent to strengthening the power of your work. You might go through steps habitually without dropping into a deep spiritual state. Your work can then lose meaning and passion. It is important to keep your work fresh. Use different ways to prepare. Change up your practice in some way so that you do not fall into a habitual routine. This is true for all of your practices. But you can easily fall into a repetitive routine with a ceremony you practice every month. You want to continue to dive deep instead of working on the surface.

THE HIDDEN REALMS

A shaman is a man or woman who shifts into an altered state of consciousness, a spiritual state of consciousness, to travel outside of time into the hidden realms that many people call non-ordinary reality. These hidden realms do exist, but we have closed the veils between the worlds and have forgotten other dimensions to life that we once we knew as children. As children we had our invisible friends who provided comfort in our lives. Through our imagination and our daydreams, we would experience other worlds beyond what appeared to us in ordinary reality. Some of us would travel to the stars and communicate with the star beings. As children many of us communicated with fairies and animal spirits. The power of our imaginations gave us greater access to the spiritual realms.

The native people in Australia call non-ordinary reality the Dreamtime. In the Celtic traditions the term the Other World is used in speaking about the non-ordinary realms. I like to use the terms *the hidden worlds, the hidden realms,* and *the invisible realms* to reflect that while these places are always present, many people no longer acknowledge their existence.

When one examines the cross-cultural stories of shamans, there are three common levels of worlds that are described. These worlds are also depicted through different forms of artwork that have been drawn on rocks and in caves around the world. The hidden worlds that the shamans travel to are known as the Underworld or Lower World, the Middle World, and the Upper World.

In both the Lower World and the Upper World, there are different levels that can be explored. The Middle World is the hidden realm of nature and the dimension we live in. In the course of this book you will be encouraged to perform shamanic journeys to the Middle World to work with nature spirits, the spirits of trees and plants, the Hidden Folk, the elements, the stars, and the moon; to access information from helping spirits in the past and future; and to even travel into parallel universes.

Abiding in these hidden realities there are helping spirits—compassionate spirits who offer their guidance. They also have the ability and capacity to heal issues that affect you on an emotional and physical level. As you will learn in part 2, your helping spirits might not perform a healing on you, but they might give you advice and show you the steps you need to take to make changes in your life that create healing. The helping spirits have great compassion for what's happening with individuals and on the planet. As you meet with your helping spirits over time, you will build a strong partnership with them.

Different helping spirits are consulted when any kind of information is needed. The helping spirits might appear as power animals and teachers in human form. There are also elemental spirits in earth, air, water, and fire that sustain life and have great wisdom and power to impart to us. Rocks and crystals are helping spirits, as are trees and plants. Many shamans work with plant spirits in order to heal a variety of ailments. There are also the Hidden Folk, who are caretakers of this great Earth and want to help us as we care for the Earth, too. Many of us call them *the fairy folk,* which includes the fairies, elves, and forest guardians. These too can appear as helping spirits for us.

ACCESSING THE HIDDEN REALMS

As people gain experience with journeying in the hidden realms, many practitioners realize that the non-ordinary realms are a hologram rather than linear worlds. You might become aware of the thinning of the veils between the ordinary and non-ordinary realms. As you learn to heighten your consciousness and open your third eye, or strong eye, as shamans do, you understand that you just have to lift a thin veil between the worlds to gain access to the hidden realms. There are many doorways to enter through.

Many people access the non-ordinary realms during their nighttime dreams. Incubating dreams was a practice in Ancient Egypt and Greece. In some native communities separate sleeping quarters were set up for dreamers who would incubate dreams for information for the community. In shamanic cultures the information received in dreams is taken very seriously. An individual might have a prophetic dream or might receive information that is important for all individuals in the community to hear.

Dreamtime is a time when you can meet up with a variety of helping spirits who might provide healing help or share with you guidance that will help you improve your life or work through a challenging issue. Before going to sleep at night, you can set your intention to ask for a dream that provides the guidance you might be needing in your life. The information you receive in your dreams assists you in your waking life.

It is common for people in indigenous communities to gather each morning to listen to each person's dreams. This is a time to reflect on the guidance shared during the night that might be important to hear for the health and well-being of not just one individual but for the community at large.

Nature itself offers a powerful doorway into the invisible realms. There are shamans who spend many hours in nature, without the use of the drum, where they meet with helping spirits, accessing great wisdom and receiving powerful visions. Years ago I had a very deep and powerful journey where I was shown that, in the beginning of time, people were taught how to heal by spending time with plants in nature. Nature will provide much healing and insight for you in how to live a healthy life. Nature is a helping spirit.

THE SHAMANIC JOURNEY

One of the major ceremonies that a shaman performs is the shamanic journey. Performing a shamanic journey is how we can use the ancient art of shamanism for practical and visionary purposes in our daily life. It is a way to meet up with helping spirits in the invisible realms to access information and gain insights on how you can improve your life or to ask for healing help. The helping spirits that you meet in the course of working with the material in *Walking in Light* will help you deepen the work to empower your daily life.

Because the practice of shamanism is a system of direct revelation, all shamans describe their experiences differently. There is no right way to experience a shamanic journey. In our culture we try to conform to the *right* way to practice. This takes away the meaning and the passion for the work. To keep the work spiritually inspired and fresh, you must remember that everyone who practices shamanic journeying has different ways of experiencing the helping spirits and the non-ordinary realms. Also, people have different ways of entering into the non-ordinary realms. That is why I offer variations on each instruction. Please do experiment and find the method that works for you.

POSITIONING YOUR BODY

When journeying, you can lie down or sit up. Some people naturally fall asleep while lying down, especially when feeling tired. You definitely want to avoid falling asleep. Sitting up can also facilitate a deeper state of concentration leading to a clear journey.

Lying or sitting down might be too constrictive for you. Many of my students dance their journeys. You might find that movement supports a clear and a deep experience as you dance or chant your journeys. One rarely sees traditional shamans lie down to journey. Most shamans dance and chant their journeys as they step fully into the invisible realms and engage with their helping spirits. Explore being more active as you perform your journeys.

Dimming the Lights to Drop the Veils between Worlds

For the experiential journeys you can place a scarf or covering over your eyes to block out the external light. This will help you to go into a deeper state. You can also close the curtains or shut the blinds in your room. Light from the outside can pull you out of your deep sensory experience as you explore the invisible realms.

Throughout Asia and in parts of South America where shamans dance their journeys, the shamans cover their eyes with a mask or headdress that has fringes covering their eyes. These eye curtains can be quite elaborate, using fur for the headband and with beads woven into the fringe. The fringe allows the shaman to be able to engage fully in the journey while being able to see where he or she is in the ordinary world. It allows the shaman to be in two worlds at the same time.

You can make a simple eye covering with fringes. You can use a bandana for this. Fold the bandana so it is in the shape of a triangle. The top will be the headband that ties around your head. Cut vertical fringes that cover your eyes. Trim the fringes so that they sit above your nose. You can do the same with a scarf. And of course you can use your creativity to make a more decorative eye covering to use.

Invoking the Power of Sound with Instruments

Playing or listening to shamanic instruments helps to heighten the level of consciousness needed to fully step into the hidden realms. The Earth loves to hear drumming, and you will find yourself feeling more connected to the land where you live and the heartbeat of the Earth as you drum or listen to a recording. Doing this will help you to maintain clarity and focus while quieting the mind chatter that oftentimes plagues people while journeying. Sometimes while journeying you might find your mind looping to *I should be answering emails. I wonder what I'm going to cook for dinner tonight.* Playing shamanic percussion for yourself will curtail these kinds of distracting thoughts and will help you concentrate and keep your focus. I work in this way. I sit up, and I drum or rattle.

As you use your drumstick, use your wrist to drum instead of using your arm. Do the same if you choose to rattle. In this way you do not have to concentrate on the motion you are making to provide the rhythm to journey to, and your arm will not get tired. Shamans use their own unique rhythms to journey to. And the rhythm can change throughout the journey marking different phases of the work. When you drum or rattle for yourself, you can allow different rhythms to emerge that support your work.

You do not have to go out and buy expensive musical instruments. In the beginning of my practice, I used a pot and a wooden spoon. I also use bottles that I have filled with pebbles, corn, and crystals. I journey frequently using a bottle of Advil as a rattle. Use your imagination and create your own shamanic instruments.

For those of you beginning your practice of shamanic journeying, you might wish to purchase a CD of drumming. Or you can download a drumming track that can be used for the exercises. In the resources section I have provided information on the shamanic drumming CDs I have recorded. Many people journey to other forms of music that were designed to facilitate a meditative state or deep relaxation. You can experiment with some of the CDs you already have at home and notice if certain music heightens and expands your state of consciousness. However, pick a piece of music that has a tempo that will keep your consciousness moving and is not so slow that it pulls you back into an ordinary state of consciousness or puts you to sleep.

During Your Journeys

In the shamanic trance you move aside your conscious mind to travel into the hidden realms. Being in a shamanic trance is not an unconscious state, but rather a state where you move into an expanded state of consciousness, shifting your focus from the ordinary everyday world and enter into the world of spirit.[1]

You are in full control of yourself while journeying. You can choose to move up or down, you can talk to the helping spirit who presents itself to you, or you can decide to walk away from it. It is always up to you when to return from the journey, and you can do so at any time during the drumming.

You are not in control of which helping spirit might volunteer to help you. For example, a journeyer might wish that an eagle presents itself as a helping spirit. But a gazelle might present itself as a helping spirit that has important teachings to share at this time. You might be surprised by how profound the advice is that you do receive instead of making up the conversation between you and a helping spirit. In this sense, shamanic journeying differs from daydreaming where you use your imagination to make up characters and the scenarios you wish to see.

During your shamanic journey you are aware of what is going on around your physical body. Your dog or cat might snuggle up to you while you are journeying, and you will feel it paws on your body. You might feel the air blowing on you from a fan or an open window. While listening to the drum, you might hear a phone ring, an airplane flying over your house, the siren of an ambulance, or a car honking. Whenever I hear a sound from my external environment, I tell myself that every sound I hear takes me deeper into my journey—and it does.

Shamanic journeying is a practice that improves over time. Be persistent! Where attention goes, energy goes. With practice you will strengthen and revitalize your access into the spiritual realms. As you proceed with your journeys, you will find a style that you settle into that works for you. Many people who journey are not aware of moving up or down into the Lower World or Upper World. Rather their intention simply brings them directly to their helping spirits. Some of my students begin by purely using their imagination to make up a scenario of journeying into the Lower, Middle, or Upper World until their brain waves shift, moving them into a new and unexpected experience.

For some people practicing shamanism, their psychic senses that are the strongest change over time. Some people initially see colorful and vivid images during their journeys. But later on they find that the images seem to lessen, and they begin to hear messages shared by helping spirits. There are times when journeyers experience being fully in a journey. And there are times when they are aware that they see themselves and the spirits from a distance. It is important to note that the quality of your journeys will change over time.

You will find your own way. Proceed with the work and don't get stuck on "the method" or belief that there is a right way to journey. Your intention will light the path for you to discover your unique way of journeying to meet with your helping spirits.

Returning from Your Journey

When journeying, you might find that sometimes you need a longer time to journey and sometimes you might need a very short time to obtain the guidance you are seeking. Everybody is unique. Some people need longer journeying times, and some people need shorter journeying times.

When it is time to return from the world you are exploring, if you use a drumming track or CD designed for shamanic journeys, there will be a return beat to let you know. When you hear the change in drumbeat, say good-bye to the helping spirit you were with and leave the landscape you have been visiting. During the rapid return beat, bring your attention back to the room while taking with you all you have gained from the experience.

If you use a drumming CD or a CD with other shamanic instruments that does not have a return beat, that is fine. When you feel your journey is complete, simply say good-bye to your helping spirit or spiritual ally, and retrace your steps back to your starting place. The same holds true if you decide to drum or rattle for yourself.

Be very disciplined with returning from your journey. You want to travel into the invisible realms with intention and then travel slowly back to the room you are in. This is essential to feeling grounded and completely present after a journey. Repeat your return if you do not feel grounded and present once back.

SURRENDER THE OUTCOME

It can be difficult to journey for yourself when you are too attached to the outcome. For this reason, in native cultures often the shaman would not journey for his or her own family members. When journeying you might find that you cannot get clear information when journeying for a spouse, partner, or your children. Or you might find that you are too worried while dealing with a physical illness to leave your ordinary world behind and step into the invisible realms. In these cases, it might be impossible to be objective and to step aside, opening to the guidance of your helping spirits. In this situation you should find an objective person to journey on your behalf. I share resources at the end of *Walking in Light* to find trained practitioners you can work with.

Walking in Light is written to teach you how to use the practice of shamanism for your own personal healing, development, and evolution. Please do not journey for somebody else without his or her permission and knowledge. Using shamanic journeys for others is not only beyond the scope of this book, but it is an ethical issue to perform shamanic divination work for another without permission. This would be akin to voyeurism.

WEAVING THE SACRED INTO THE ORDINARY

As you learn to live your life as a ceremony and attune yourself to an ongoing connection with your helping spirits, you will find that you can divine information during your daily activities.

Through intention you can call your helping spirits to be with you for protection while you are doing such activities as driving. You can call upon the help of the compassionate spirits to protect your boundaries so that others do not psychically impact you when working with people in the public realm. You do not need to perform a formal journey to ask your spirits to surround you with protection and fill you with power. You just have to ask for the help to be given.

There are situations where you might not take time out of your daily activities to perform a formal journey, but the veils between the worlds open, and your helping spirit travels into the Middle World and shares an important message. You might find that if needed, you receive spiritual assistance while you are at work. For example, you might find yourself at a business meeting and you hear a helping spirit whispering into your ear just the right words to say to transform a challenging conversation. This is one example of how a helping spirit might make contact with you at work without the need for a journey.

Whenever you perform an activity that creates a quiet meditative state, spiritual guidance can bubble up. You might notice when you do the dishes, sweep and vacuum, or engage in a craft that these actions create a spaciousness and change your brain waves, where you have access to your helping spirits.

Although you will find that you can weave the sacred into your daily routine, you must also remember to stay disciplined with the work. The practice of shamanism is a discipline where a shaman knows the difference between ordinary reality and non-ordinary reality. Driving is a not a time to do your shamanic work. Although some people find that driving can create a meditative state, it is a time for you to focus on the road and other drivers. You need to make sure that you are fully present while doing certain tasks in your life and you are not having what is called a *bleed through* from the other realms.

Just remember to keep to the discipline and only journey when it is physically safe for yourself and others to do so. You want to remain grounded and present in the ordinary realms while driving, walking in traffic, or using heavy machinery.

It will be most interesting to watch the evolution of shamanism practiced by future generations as consciousness evolves over time.

2

Gathering Your Tools
for Ceremony

WORKING WITH THE SHAMANIC PATH as a visionary experience requires you to separate from your ordinary distractions and preoccupations of the mind and step into the world of the sacred. There are tools that can help you move into an expanded state of consciousness and create sacred space. These tools help to prepare you mentally, emotionally, and physically to leave your ordinary world behind so you can enter fully into your visionary experience. And there are also tools to help you return and feel grounded when you complete your shamanic journey. Shamans often use physical and psychological tools to shift their consciousness to enter into the hidden realms. Some shamans fast or go out into the wilderness and do a vision quest. There are shamans who use vision plants where they are led into the hidden realms through the use of a hallucinogen. Some shamans chant and dance for long periods of time, creating a state where the ordinary realm of existence is left behind. In this way they can travel deeply into the invisible realms. In this chapter, I share some tools with you to help deepen your shamanic experience.

YOUR SENSE PERCEPTIONS AS TOOLS

The most potent tool for you to use in your shamanic work is your sensory awareness. It is important to use all of your senses while journeying. Journeying is not an out-of-body experience. A Hopi friend of mine says that when the Hopi people journey, they take their bodies with them. This is true for shamans in traditional cultures.

By shifting consciousness, the shaman lifts the veil between the visible and invisible realms and steps into a different dimension of reality. The shaman is in this world with all his or her senses activated. He or she sees, hears, feels, smells, and tastes just as we would in our daily life. The shaman walks up to helping spirits and engages with them as we might when we meet with a friend, family member, loved one, or business partner.

In the modern world we have deadened our senses. We watch images that are presented to us on the screen, and most of us no longer use our imagination to truly focus on the rich visual awareness we are capable of. We live and work in environments where the air can be stale. Many people use scented candles and artificial fragrant sprays that are made with chemicals to cover up how the air smells. Many today listen to music on devices throughout the day. When was the last time you heard a tree singing? Trees do sing, and if you open your "invisible ears," you will hear them. We love to hear bird songs, but many of us have stopped listening. We cover up the true taste of our foods with artificial flavorings. And many of us who live in urban environments are so flooded with sensory stimulation that we have learned to shut down and don't always experience the beauty of the world around us.

A friend of mine was sharing with me her experience on a boat trip on a river in a rural part of Australia. The guide on the boat was pointing out a tree in the distance with a snake on it. The people in the boat could barely see the tree that the guide was pointing to. As they got closer everyone could see the tree and the snake and were amazed at how the guide could see them so far away. I do not believe that the guide had extraordinary vision. It is more likely that the guide had developed and enlivened his senses by living in the natural world.

Before an earthquake or other natural disasters occur, animal behavior changes significantly. During a destructive tidal wave in Thailand, animals had moved to higher ground and to safety before the tidal wave was apparent to humans. Most humans have deadened their psychic senses and do not pick up on the messages that animals receive. The senses of nature beings are heightened enough to pick up changes occurring in the earth and in the environment.

We are allowing our senses to atrophy. We simply do not use them in the way that our brain is capable of. We miss much of the beauty in ordinary reality, but we also do not experience the depth of the mystical and magical realms that the shaman journeys into. Some of us remain too passive and don't engage our senses in a way that brings us fully into the hidden worlds.

To take a more active role in your journeys, you must open up to your sensory awareness. When I use the word *experience* throughout *Walking in Light*, notice what you are sensing. Here are some examples:

Does your nose tickle when you breathe in a fragrance while you are traveling in the hidden realms?

What is the quality of your heartbeat—is it beating quickly in anticipation and excitement, or does it slow down as you relax into the journey?

Does your mouth feel dry as you explore a new adventure in non-ordinary reality?

Are your feet or hands cold or warm?

Do they tingle as you explore a new landscape?

Are your shoulders relaxed, or do they feel tight?

Do you see the light shining brightly?

What images do you see? Notice the colors.

Do you notice a wealth of sound created by the wind and animal life?

Are you fully breathing in the fragrance of the earth and
the plant life?

Does the air taste salty or earthy?

What does the texture of the landscape you are standing
in feel like to your fingers?

Stepping into your full sensory awareness will bring you deeper into
your journey so that you become actively engaged in the invisible
realms. We live in a culture that emphasizes the visual sense. Many
people who embark on the practice of shamanic journeying want to
watch TV or a movie. We want to take on a passive role and have
images provided to us on a screen, but the true art of shamanic journeying requires you to be more active. We can get so caught up in the
visual and verbal messages from our helping spirits that we stop looking for the deeper meaning they are trying to share with us.

At first when you journey, you might find one invisible psychic
sense more active than another. I tend to be clairaudient. I *hear* my
helping spirits speaking to me. Some people are clairsentient where
they *feel* the information in their bones. This is a deep and powerful way to receive spiritual information. But in this culture, where
you are trained to focus on images in the outside world, you have to
train yourself to go inside and notice what senses are strongest for you
during a journey.

As you continue to journey, focus on enlivening all your invisible
senses so that you see, hear, feel, taste, and even smell the fragrances
of the invisible world. It is just as if you are walking in an ordinary
state of consciousness in nature. You would not just want to *see*
the landscape you are in as some of the richness of being in nature
is hearing the sounds and breathing in and smelling the rich fragrances. You want to feel your fingers touch the textures of the earth.
Allow yourself to open up *all* of your senses as you move forward
with your journeys.

INSTRUMENTS AND MUSIC

To open the veils between the ordinary and non-ordinary realms and travel into the hidden realms where shamans meet with their helping spirits, some form of percussion, especially drumming or rattling, is used. Rhythmic drumming and rattling shifts the shaman into a heightened level of consciousness where his or her free soul can travel into the invisible realms. In some cultures shamans use sticks or bells. In Australia the shamans use the didgeridoo and click sticks that are often painted with beautiful and intricate designs.

The Sami shamans of Lapland and Norway use drumming, but they also use monotonous chanting called *joiking*. In northern Scandinavia, the Christian missionaries took away and burned the Sami shamans' drums and banned their use. Some families hid the drums or buried them for safekeeping. The Sami people developed their own form of chanting, or joiking, in times when they no longer had access to their drums.

Scientific research has shown that when we are in an ordinary state of consciousness, our thinking state, and only perceiving the tangible world we live in, our brain waves are in a beta state. When a shaman or a shamanic practitioner listens to a rhythmic or a monotonous drumbeat, the brain waves slow down. First the brain waves slow down to an alpha state, which is a light meditative state of consciousness. Then they slow down into a deeper state called a theta state. Once in the theta state the shaman's free soul journeys into the invisible realms allowing access to helping spirits. As one's brain waves continue to slow down, a delta state is reached. This is the state we enter when we go to sleep and dream.

PREPARATION AS A TOOL

With the practice of shamanism you must shift into a heightened level of consciousness before performing any ceremony to travel into the invisible realms. Most important is the preparation you do before you engage in the spiritual work. By doing this you will experience clear and profound journeys. Traditionally, shamans would fast and vision quest before their ceremonial journey work. In our modern culture we try to dive into the spiritual realms without taking the time to shift from our mental thoughts that follow us throughout the day. We go from talking on the phone, answering our emails, or straight from work into journeying into the imaginal realms. And then we wonder why we do not have a clear, deep, and powerful experience.

It is crucial to separate yourself from the activities you were doing before and focus on the practice that lies ahead. Set aside appropriate times when you can focus on your spiritual work. You want to create time and space where you can go into the depth of your experience and not be distracted by daily ordinary concerns. The phrase I use for preparing to do your shamanic work is "creating a state of spaciousness." I am not suggesting that you fast or vision quest before beginning each journey. But you need to create space.

Do this little exercise to experience the difference a little preparation can make. Take a minute and close your eyes and take a few deep breaths. Imagine trying to have a deep spiritual experience while you are boxed in by your daily thoughts and the structure of your ordinary life. Now imagine pushing the mental boxes that confine you away so that there is a clear field around you where you can access a spiritual state of consciousness. When you feel you have the experience of what "spaciousness" can bring to you, open your eyes.

Think about a ship that's preparing to sail out to sea. Before that ship can sail, it must pull up the anchor. The preparation work that shamans do before performing spiritual practices is a way to pull up the anchor in order to sail away into the vast landscape of the invisible realms. Here are some ways to do this:

Plan on journeying during times of the day when your mind is clear. Some people find that they have clearer journeys for themselves in the morning, and for some the best time is right before they drift off to sleep at night.

Taking a short walk in nature before journeying will clear your mind.

Other ways to clear your mind include meditating, singing, dancing, movement, or breathing deeply.

Find another physical activity you can engage in before doing your spiritual work such as some form of physical exercise, tai chi, chi gong, or yoga.

These are a few ideas that will help you open your physical channel and raise your energy and vibration to leave the ordinary world behind as you step into the non-ordinary realms. Shamans become a "hollow bone" or "empty reed" where they open themselves up to be a true vessel of spirit.

POWER SONGS

Shamans drum, dance, and sing sometimes for many hours as they prepare to become a vessel for the energy of the helping spirits. Shamans have power songs that they sing before their ceremonial work. I sing a power song that I was given while I was out in nature. I only sing this song before performing healing work. When I start to sing, I immediately feel my ego, or personality, stepping aside and my connection with my helping spirits becoming deep and clear.

To obtain your own power song, start to drum or rattle. Begin by humming. Next you might start chanting. Allow your soul to sing. A traditional way to find a power song is to go into nature and sit with a tree. Again notice if a song or chant starts to bubble up from deep within.

Let go of all your judgments about what your song sounds like, your beliefs about the quality of your voice, and your ability to sing. All life sings. It is your birthright to express your soul through song, adding to the universal song of life.

ALTARS

You can set up an altar in a space where you perform your shamanic work. This creates sacred space providing a path between the visible and invisible realms. On a table or on the floor, place a special piece of cloth or a small rug. Place on the cloth or rug some crystals or stones from nature, some flowers, or even a candle you can burn when doing sacred work. Creating sacred space supports your spiritual work. Some people like to burn sacred herbs such as sage, cedar, or sweet grass. You can find incense that assists in supporting a sacred state of consciousness.

I replace certain things on my altar with new sacred objects when I feel I need a reflection of a major shift I have made in my life. My altar changes as I change.

Go to your altar when you are sending out prayers or asking for healing. I place names of people who are asking for help on my altar. I return to my altar during times when I need some comfort.

INTENTION AND PHRASING
QUESTIONS ARE TOOLS

Throughout *Walking in Light* you will be encouraged to pose certain questions and intentions to your helping spirits. I do want to share some advice in asking questions in your shamanic journey. Avoid asking questions that begin with *when*. You are journeying outside of time, and time takes on a different meaning in the invisible realms. I would not ask a question such as, "When should I leave my job?"

Asking "why" questions might not lead to a satisfactory answer. Asking why a tragedy occurred where so many innocent people were killed might not be answered by your helping spirits. Sometimes we need to learn how to accept and embrace the mysteries of life.

I steer people away from yes-no questions. The spirits see everything that happens in your life as an adventure. You might receive a yes answer in asking if you should marry someone or if you should move to a new house or city. There might be painful and unnecessary challenges ahead if you move forward with your decision, but the spirits see this as part of your learning. They might respond with, "Sure! Go for it!"

When you are journeying on your own personal questions, phrase your questions so that you get the most detailed information possible. In this way, *you* can make the right decision for yourself. Asking a question such as, "What will I learn if I move forward with this marriage or move?" will give you guidance that can inform your choice.

A powerful intention to journey with is by beginning your sentence with "show me . . ." In this way your spirits are now free to answer you by showing you omens as you go about your day. The helping spirits might put people on your path who show you the way. They reveal answers during your everyday life that truly show you the next steps to take for your healing and as an answer to a question you have, or the helping spirits might show you images within your journey that will provide you with the insight you are seeking.

Although I am sharing guidance with you about phrasing questions, experience is the best teacher. Relax into the work and let your own experience lead you into new levels of communication with your helping spirits.

INTERPRETATION AS A TOOL TO END YOUR CEREMONY

Over time you will learn how to interpret your journeys. The helping spirits tend to share their guidance and wisdom through showing you metaphorical symbols or sharing metaphorical answers. They often do not answer a question in a linear fashion only speaking to your rational mind. When you have completed your journey, reflect on how the guidance you received can be a metaphorical answer. Take your time with this as the helping spirits plant seeds with their answers that will grow into plants of wisdom over time.

Sometimes the helping spirits do this by role-playing and acting out a scenario where they are attempting to show you that you need rest or you need to address an issue such as fear, disappointment, or anger. Or you might watch as the spirits fight with each other. I have heard students share that their power animal is tired or is feeling ill. The helping spirits do not have physical bodies; therefore, they do not get tired or ill—they are literally showing you personal issues that need to be examined.

KEEPING A JOURNAL

You can keep a journal of your journeys and dreams as a way to record your experiences for future review. But remember the helping spirits are showing ways to improve your life. Journeys are not just for collecting information. You might find that until you use some of the information shared with you in your divination work, you do not get further information from your helping spirits. You don't always need to agree with your helping spirits, as making choices how to live is your ultimate responsibility, but you do need to work with the guidance given.

Journaling after you complete a ceremony will help you to return fully to your ordinary state of consciousness. While writing out your experience, you might find insights bubbling up from deep within. As you reflect on and review your notes over time, you might find a new deeper interpretation emerging.

Another way you can use a journal is visual—you can draw symbols that might emerge from your journeywork. Recording journeys through artwork and drawing or painting symbols is a powerful way to end your ceremony.

TOOLS TO WORK WITH EGO
AND CONDITIONING

By continuing to do personal work, you will learn to distinguish messages that you desire to hear versus what is truly coming from the helping spirits. Our ego can get in the way of our spiritual work. I encourage all students of shamanism to engage in some type of psychological exploration to continue to identify and work on egoic states that might interfere with going deep into the world of spirit.

People new to the practice of journeying often ask, "Am I making up the information, the guidance, and healing my helping spirits are sharing with me?" This question is common for those who grew up in a family where the invisible realms were not talked about or supported. Most of us were told, "Stop dreaming. Stop using your imagination. Wake up, behave, and conform. If you don't stand out, if you don't shine your light too brightly, you will fit in and get by in life." So many of us have sacrificed our own creative ability and our own imaginal gifts to tap into those inner realms that we were able to enter into as children.

If mind chatter is interfering with your journey, come back and engage in more preparation work. Sing, dance, or take a time out to walk in nature and clear your mind. If you keep hearing a looping thought such as *I am just making this all up,* agree with your mind. In this way you do not waste all your time in the journey fighting with yourself. Just agree and move on. Or, I find asking a "what if" question is quite effective to quiet the mind. Ask yourself the question, "What if I am not making this up?" In spiritual traditions it is taught that the world is a dream. In truth we are making our world up. Using our imagination is how we dream our world into being.

You might find that your body helps you experience the truth of your experience. Do you feel the truth of your experience in your bones? Learn how to identify what it feels like in your body when you are having a deep, truthful, and meaningful experience. My spirits use different vocabulary than I use. When I hear the words and tonation of my helping spirits, I know I am in a deep state.

TOOLS FOR GROUNDING

After completing your shamanic journeywork or ceremonial work, if you feel spacey, disoriented, agitated, or emotional for no identifiable reason, it means that you are not grounded in your body and have not returned fully into an ordinary state of consciousness. Please do not get into a car and drive anywhere until you feel fully grounded.

Fully returning to your body and to the physical world can be accomplished by paying attention to how you do it. Once your shamanic journey feels complete and you are ready to return, take some time to thank your helping spirits you were visiting and to say goodbye. This tells your psyche that your journey is ending. Then walk back with discipline by slowly retracing your steps. If you come back too quickly leading to a state of feeling ungrounded, go back into the journey and repeat your return. You can do this by listening to the CD you were journeying with. You can also drum or rattle for yourself. I often tell my students to use two rocks or two sticks to click together to repeat a return beat for oneself.

When completing a ceremony that you perform whether it is simple or more complex, you can also thank the helping spirits you worked with. State that the ceremony is done for now. This is a way of ending where you honor the helping spirits while also making a clear indication to your psyche that the work is complete. This will help you to feel more grounded at the end of your work. Here are some additional ways to ground:

You can imagine yourself sitting with a tree in nature. Close your eyes and take some slow deep breaths. With your imagination lean back and feel the bark of the tree. Feel the power and strength of the deep roots growing down into the earth. Feel your connection with the earth and your body as you do this.

You can also take a walk in nature while focusing on connecting with the earth and to your body with each step that you take.

If you find that you have an ongoing issue with feeling ungrounded after your shamanic work, perform a journey and ask one of your helping spirits for a practice that you can perform at the end of your work to help you feel connected to your body and the earth.

LAUGHTER

Have patience with yourself as you explore which doorways into the invisible realms work best for you. Engage your sense of humor. Shamans laugh a lot. It's not that they don't take life seriously. They do, but humor helps keep them centered and balanced as they witness the challenges in the world. Humor also lights up the path into the inner worlds as you delve into the deep, beautiful, rich places where guidance and healing is waiting for you.

TOOLS TO MEASURE RESULTS

Over time you will learn to trust your helping spirits. Trust comes with experience. You cannot force trust. Observe your results: Did the guidance you received in your journey help you in your life? If you received a healing in your journey, do you notice a change in how you feel? In the end it is important to observe the results of your shamanic journey work. Shamanism has always been a practice that is based on getting good results. If the shaman could not heal the people or divine food sources, the people in the community would die. As you journey notice whether the guidance you receive works for you to improve the quality of your life. Here are some examples of results I have witnessed:

Suzanne was dealing with a high level of anxiety that prevented her from fully engaging in and enjoying life. Through her ongoing journeys and following the steps her helping spirit suggested, she learned how to surrender to the joy of life as an adventure.

John learned how to shift his anger toward his boss and create a harmonious relationship with him that created more peace in his life.

Theresa gained tools to improve her health by following the guidance shared from her helping spirit.

David learned how to focus his energies to create a life that had meaning for him.

Joy was able to bring peaceful and healthful communication into her troubled relationship with her husband.

Peter was able to forgive himself for his past actions and to learn the power of self-love.

Heather learned how to feel empowered by the spiritual practices she engaged in and to believe in herself.

As you proceed with your shamanic work, over time you will find that the guidance and healing you receive can help you in many areas of your life.

PART 2

COMPASSIONATE, HELPING SPIRITS *and* SPIRITUAL ALLIES

TAKE A FEW DEEP BREATHS AND GET COMFORTABLE. Think about a favorite place in nature that you enjoy visiting. This is a place of beauty, a place where you can relax and feel calm. It is a sacred place for you. Now imagine yourself in this place of peace and healing. Close your eyes and breathe deeply. Notice how your energy flows through your body. Place your hands on your heart and feel your heart opening with each breath in and breath out. Breathe out any disturbing thoughts and breathe in love. Breathe all the way down into your abdomen. Send the energy of your breath to any part of your body that feels tense and release the tension as you exhale. Notice the thoughts, feelings, sensations, and images that arise as you breathe. Notice the sounds around you as you breathe in and breathe out. And as you continue to breathe deeply, take a step back and leave your everyday life behind you for now.

Experience yourself standing in this sacred landscape as fully as you can right now. Open your senses to take in the beauty of the landscape you are standing in. Look around you:

What plant life is here?

Are there any animals?

Are there any rocks or minerals?

Is there a body of water?

What is the quality of earth like?

Are you in the mountains, or in a forest, in the desert, or on a beach?

Is the sun shining?

Are there clouds in the sky? What is the color of the sky?

What are all the colors surrounding you? Drink in all the colors with your eyes.

Feel yourself fully present in this landscape. Feel the earth beneath you.

Feel the air on your skin. Is it warm or is it cold? Is the air moist or is it dry? Is the air still, are you being caressed by gentle breezes, or is the wind blowing strong?

Listen to the sounds of nature. Do you hear the sounds of any water, birdcalls, or animal noises? Do you hear the wind?

Take a very deep breath and breathe in the wonderful clean and fresh fragrances of this peaceful place. The fragrances might be ones you have smelled before bringing back happy memories, or they might be new to you.

Feel yourself absorbing the life-giving light of the sun into all your cells. Feel the emotions that arise from being in such a sacred place filled with peace and beauty. Open your heart and feel love, peace, and gratitude within.

As you open to your sensory awareness, experience your mind quieting and your energy expanding. Experience the peace and healing of this place. You are held in the loving arms of the power of the universe and life itself. You are not alone; you are part of a greater whole. The Earth has a heartbeat, and as you breathe deeply, you experience yourself becoming one with her heartbeat. As you feel the beat of your heart like the rhythm of a drumbeat, feel your heart pulse with love and gratitude for the beauty of nature and all it shares with you.

Begin by honoring the directions.

Honor and greet the East. The East represents the spring. It is the place of the rising sun always reminding you of new beginnings and the chance of unlimited possibilities.

Honor and greet the South, the season of summer. Give thanks for the protection you receive as you live your life from a state of love. The South can represent the direction of intuition and living from a state of awe and wonder as you did as a child.

Honor and greet the West, the season of autumn and the direction of the setting sun. The West teaches you about the power of death and rebirth. There is always the new that comes from letting go of what no longer serves you.

Honor and greet the North, the season of winter. Give thanks for the wisdom that is shared from your ancestral spirits.

Honor and greet the sky above and the earth below, and acknowledge that you bridge the great powers of Heaven and Earth through your open heart. Honor your inner divine spirit that is a reflection of the creator.

Next give thanks to the spirit of the Earth who provides you with beauty and the nurturance to thrive.

Feel gratitude for the living being we call air, which is the first living being who welcomed you into the world as you took your first breath. Air is your constant companion as you are always in connection with it as you breathe. And air teaches you about your connection with all of life as you share some of your DNA when you breathe out and breathe in the DNA of others.

Send your gratitude to water. There is no life without water. Water held you while you were growing in your mother's womb and then escorted you into the world. Water fills your cells with life-giving nurturance.

Greet and give thanks to the sun for the energy you need to thrive. The sun reminds you of the passion for life and reflects back to you the divine light that shines within. The sun is a teacher of unconditional giving, for it gives without asking for anything in return.

Honor, greet, and give thanks to the moon and the stars for sharing beauty and wisdom and for providing you with guidance. You honor the moon and stars by shining your light, reflecting the beauty of the night sky.

Breathe out love to all the living beings who live in the elements, the spirit that lives in all things. Honor the animals, birds, insects, fish, reptiles, trees, plants, minerals, and rocks.

Honor, greet, and give thanks to the spirit of the helping ancestors who have sacrificed much so that you may live a life filled with peace, harmony, love, light, and abundance.

Acknowledge, honor, greet, and give thanks to the Hidden Folk who are the fairies, elves, little people, and forest guardians who remind you of the magic of life. These nature spirits caretake the Earth and love it so. Give thanks to the Spirit of the Land where you live for providing you with a home.

Give thanks to all the helping spirits who continue to share their wisdom, healing, and unconditional love. Give thanks to them for lighting your path, leading to a deep, rich, and joyful life.

Gently feel yourself coming back from your experience into the room you are in. Notice how you are feeling right now. Give thanks to the spirits and give thanks for your life.

3

Power Animals, Guardians, Teachers, *and* Ancestral Helping Spirits

THE ASPECT OF YOURSELF that is a personality is playing and engaging in the game of life. Your helping spirits are in the audience. They have a different view or perspective they can share with you. They can work in partnership with us and in the spirit of cooperation and collaboration to be in service to the planet at this time. You will learn that your helping spirits love you unconditionally, and when you are held in such love, you begin to learn how to love yourself unconditionally. This leads you to make decisions and take actions of loving-kindness toward yourself and others.

The helping spirits can provide healing on behalf of others and for the Earth itself. It is the responsibility of all of us to do our personal work and open up our awareness to a new way of leading life where healing comes naturally. Before the helping spirits can assist in healing the Earth, we need to learn how to live in a more responsible fashion and make decisions that honor the Earth and the nature beings who share it with us. The helping spirits do not have a body or a personality. They are formless energies that show us a form as it provides comfort for our ego. But as long as we attach form to the helping spirits, we put them in "a box," and we limit their power. This is a conversation for later on in *Walking in Light*. For now I am simply planting a seed of wisdom that grows beyond form.

In shamanic cultures it's believed that when we are born, the spirit of at least one power animal or guardian spirit volunteers to remain with us to keep us healthy on emotional and physical levels and to protect us from harm. You might be familiar with the concept of guardian angels, which is similar to the role of your power animals and *guardian spirits,* which is another term to use instead of *power animal.* However, your guardian spirits will not stand in the way of your life's lessons. Life is Earth school, and you go through many adventures and challenges that support growth and evolution. Your power animals and guardian spirits will be with you every step of the way, holding you in love as you go through turbulent times. Your helping spirit might appear as another type of nature spirit such as an insect, a tree, or the sun.

When you meet up with a power animal or guardian spirit, you will experience it as an individual, but it is important to remember that you actually have the whole species supporting you. For example, you don't work with *an* eagle, snake, or spider. You work with Eagle, Snake, or Spider. The whole species shares its power with you.

The identity of the power animal or helping spirit might surprise you. We often limit our imaginations and think about connecting with certain nature spirits as helping spirits that are spoken about in popular culture. I have students who have profound journeys with such creatures as an octopus, clam, or mouse as their helping spirit.

You might meet a mythological creature who will introduce itself to you as a power animal. Since shamanism dates back many thousands of years, we have to ask which came first, myth or the shamanic journey? Pegasus might show up as a power animal. Some people meet a now-extinct animal that introduces itself as a power animal. I hear many stories of a dinosaur or a stegosaurus showing itself as a power animal. The body of an animal can be killed, but not its spirit.

Many people meet teams of power animals. Sometimes people report, "I journeyed to ask to meet my power animal or guardian spirit and a whole group circled me." Once you state your intention or pose a question, one power animal or one helping spirit steps forth in order to answer the question or provide the healing help needed.

I suggest that you do not look up the meaning of what your power animal symbolizes in a book, rather ask why it came into your life. Power animals and guardian spirits have individual gifts to share with you. When you look up the meaning of a power animal in a book, you might miss the unique gift that a helping spirit is bringing into your life. Shamanism is a practice of direct revelation. If you want to know the gifts and teachings of your power animal, ask it.

Please note that power animals and guardian spirits live both in the Lower and Upper Worlds. In your first journey you will meet a helping spirit in the Lower World. But later on you can also journey to the Upper World to repeat the same intention.

JOURNEY TO THE LOWER WORLD TO MEET A POWER ANIMAL OR GUARDIAN SPIRIT

The intention of this journey is to travel into the Lower World to meet your power animal or guardian spirit. To demonstrate the stages of journeying, in these first few journeys I have divided the process into preparation, beginning, middle, and end.

Preparation
Darken the room you are in, or put something over your eyes after you find a place to lie down or a place to sit or stand for the journey. Disconnect your phone so you will not be disturbed. Prepare to play a drumming or other musical track you want to listen to. Or sit with your drum or rattle.

Beginning
Take some deep breaths experiencing your breath flowing through you. As you breathe deeply, notice any thoughts, sensations, and images that come up as you breathe. Notice sounds around you. Take a step back from these thoughts and sounds, and leave your everyday life behind.

To enter into the Lower World, first you will begin by starting in a place in nature. Take some time and reflect on a beautiful and sacred landscape that you enjoy visiting. Bring yourself fully into your sacred landscape. Remember journeying is not an out-of-body experience. You are not watching a movie. Step fully into this place of great beauty where you can begin your travels. Look around you and take in all the colors and sights. Listen to the sounds of nature. Take a deep breath and, breathing in, smell the fresh fragrances. Feel the quality of the air on your skin. Notice if the air feels moist or dry. Feel the temperature of the air on your skin. Feel the richness and texture of the earth. Taste the air. Take in *all* the beauty, experience *all* the elements, and be here now.

Middle

Once standing in this place, use your senses to locate a natural opening into the earth. The Lower World is typically reached by journeying through a tunnel or portal that leads into the earth. This world seems earthy and tangible and is characterized by caves, seas, dense jungles, forests, and deserts. The beings inhabiting the Lower World are the spirits of animals, trees, plants, rocks, other nature beings as well as humanlike spirits that are connected to the mysteries of the Earth.

You can travel down a tree trunk into the Lower World. You might find an opening as you walk through the entrance of a cave. You can dive into a body of water such as a lake, a river, a stream, or the ocean. You can use a waterfall as an entrance to the Lower World. Entering through a volcano can be a portal into the invisible realms. You can even enter the Lower World through a hole in the ground.

As you walk through the entrance into the earth, you will travel down a path. The path might be dark and moist. It might be filled with roots that you can grab onto as you continue to travel down. Feel your feet on the ground beneath you. Is it soft, hard, smooth, or bumpy? Smell the fragrance of the earth. Touch the earth and feel the sensations in your fingers and hands as you do this. Taste the earth. As you move through the dark earth you might notice a light at the end of a tunnel you are in.

Do not force the journey, but rather relax into it. Breathing and listening to drumming or other shamanic instruments will bring you back to center if distracting thoughts interfere with your experience. While you are traveling through your tunnel, focus on the intention that you wish to meet your power animal or guardian spirit who has volunteered to help and support you through the adventures in your life.

Once you emerge from your tunnel, open all your senses to experience the landscape you are in. Notice how fast your heart is beating. Feel the quality of the air as you breathe it in. Feel your body and notice any feelings of excitement or tension. Feel your feet in connection with the earth. Are you standing on leaves, or grass, or sand, or maybe another quality of the earth?

Notice if a power animal or guardian spirit is waiting to greet you. Again the helping spirit that meets you might not be an animal. It might be an insect, a tree, an element, or another nature being volunteering to assist you. Open yourself to the unlimited possibilities as the power of the universe provides the support of a nature spirit who loves you unconditionally.

Feel your excitement as you step closer to this nature spirit and introduce yourself. Ask this being if it is your guardian spirit. Open all your invisible senses as you discover how your guardian spirit communicates with you. Some spirits will speak to you and give you a message. This message might come through telepathic communication. You need to open your invisible ears to hear what your helping spirit is saying. You might feel the message in your body as a strong knowing that feels true and touches you on a cellular level. Some helping spirits will take you somewhere on the journey and through sitting, walking, or traveling with them, they might show you a sign. Sometimes the spirits *show us* what we need to learn rather than *tell us* through verbal messages.

Open your visual awareness, look around you, and take in all the colors and sights of the landscape you are in. Look up at the sky. Listen to the beautiful sounds of nature. Notice the sound of the water if water is in the landscape. You might hear birds singing or the sounds of insects or other animals. Feel the texture of the earth. Smell the lovely fragrances.

As you open all your senses to fully experience the beauty of the landscape, continue to get to know your helping spirit. Communicate with each other as you would with an old friend after many years of not seeing each other. You might sit or walk in silence with your helping spirit, feeling a love and connection that is beyond words. This silence brings a sense of peace and comfort.

As you develop your communication skills with your helping spirit, you can ask it any question that you are seeking guidance for. You can ask your helping spirit what it has to teach you. A bird might teach you how to rise above your situation to get a new perspective. A tree might teach you how to be more grounded. An ant might teach you how to focus on details. These are just some examples of the unlimited teachings you can receive.

As you continue your shamanic journey and you have more time to explore the different realms of the Lower World, you will find new openings to enter into. Finding a new entrance will lead you to new levels down. As you explore more levels, you will travel to different landscapes with other helping spirits available to provide assistance and support in your life.

Ending

When it is time to return, say thank you and good-bye to your guardian spirit. Before leaving, ask your helping spirit what strength it holds. Ask what gifts this spirit has to share with you. Ask your power animal or guardian spirit to touch your hands as it shares its energy and power.

Once back in your starting place in nature, take a few deep, grounding breaths. Place your hands on your heart and feel the power of your heartbeat and life-force. Next bring your consciousness back into the room you are in. If you have placed something over your eyes to block out the light, remove it. Open your eyes and feel yourself present now.

Reflect on your experience, and if you wish, you can take some notes or draw a picture so you can remember all that occurred in your journey. By taking notes while your experience is still fresh, you will have a record that you can refer to when you need a reminder of any messages shared or experiences that you have had.

TEACHERS IN HUMAN FORM

Shamans also work with teachers in human forms. In traditional shamanic cultures these were typically seen as the gods and the goddesses of a culture, religious figures, or helping ancestral spirits.

In both the Lower and Upper Worlds there are human spirits that may take the form of a god or goddess, a helping ancestral spirit, a religious figure, an ascended master, an angelic force, or legendary figure. Sometimes a mirror appears in front of your eyes signifying that you are your teacher.

JOURNEY TO THE UPPER WORLD TO MEET A TEACHER

Set your intention to travel into the Upper World to meet a teacher in human form.

Preparation

Prepare for the journey and clear your mind. Let go of ordinary concerns. Darken the room or place an eye cover over your eyes. Disconnect your phone. Set up the shamanic music you wish to use for your journey or find the drum or rattle you will be using.

The Upper World is experienced by many as more ethereal than the Lower World. The lighting might be brighter and can go from pastels, to gray, to complete darkness. In these regions, many encounter crystal cities and cities made of clouds. People may encounter a variety of helping spirits who have much to teach.

Take some deep, cleansing breaths. Place your hands on your heart or your belly to feel the power of your breath. Notice the thoughts, images, feelings, and sensations that come up as you breathe. Notice the sounds around you. As you breathe at your own pace, take a step back and leave your everyday life behind you for now.

Continue to breathe deeply and experience yourself in a special place in nature. It does not need to be the same place where you started your travels into the Lower World, but it can be. Wake up, enliven your senses, and fully experience yourself being in this place. Look around you, listening to the sounds of nature. Smell the fragrances, feel the earth, and taste the air. It is important to experience yourself fully at your starting place. This will help to fuel your journey into the Upper World.

Beginning

As you listen to the drumming or other shamanic instrument, notice if a way to the Upper World presents itself. Shamans might use the tree of life to journey down the roots into the Lower World or up the trunk and branches into the Upper World. Other traditional ways of traveling into the Upper World are climbing a rope or ladder, jumping off a mountain, riding up on a tornado or whirlwind, climbing over a rainbow, or traveling up the smoke of a fire or chimney. A bird or the guardian spirit you met in the Lower World can escort you to the Upper World.

Once your way up is clear, begin traveling up, continuing past stars and planets. Feel yourself in flight. Focus on your intention that you wish to meet a teacher in human form in the Upper World. You will find yourself at a transition that might appear as a layer of fog or clouds. The transition might appear as a skin membrane that you just have to pop through.

Middle

Step onto the first level of the Upper World. As you did in your journey into the Lower World, use your senses to fully experience the landscape you are now in. Notice if there is someone waiting to greet you. When you meet a helping being ask: "Are you my teacher? What do you have to teach me right now? Do you have a message to share with me or something to show me?"

Notice how your teacher communicates with you. You might hear his or her voice. Or you might sense that someone of great power and wisdom is with you. As you did with your guardian spirit in the Lower World, take some time to get to know your teacher.

There are many levels to explore in the Upper World. You can discover new levels in this journey or at another time.

Ending

When you hear the change in drumbeat or when you feel ready, thank your teacher for any guidance that you have received, knowing that you will return to this teacher many times, possibly for many years. Ask your teacher if he or she has a strength or gift to share with you. Allow your teacher to transmit and pass this strength to you through your hands. Take with you all you have gained from this experience and journey back knowing that this experience will create positive benefits in your life.

Journey back down through the transition, back down through the planets and stars to your starting place in nature. Return into the room where you began. Take a deep breath. If you have something covering your eyes, remove it. Reflect on the journey with your teacher, reflect on who showed up to be your teacher, and if you choose, take some notes on your experience.

Notice how your journeys to the Lower World and the Upper World were different. Reflect on the different qualities of the worlds you visited. You will learn from experience when to journey to your power animal or guardian spirit and when to journey to your teacher. In both the Lower and Upper Worlds, there are power animals, guardian spirits, and teachers in human form. As you continue your practice of shamanic journeying, you can journey to the Lower World to meet up with a teacher and to the Upper World to meet up with a power animal or guardian spirit.

OUR ANCESTORS ARE SPIRITUAL ALLIES

In shamanic cultures it has always been important to honor one's ancestors. Your ancestors also provide support and guidance in your life. Your ancestors *gave* you life. They really care about your health and well-being and the success of your efforts to manifest your dreams. They want to help further you along your path.

In a psychologically sophisticated Western culture, we often focus on what we did not get from our family. Some of us only look at how our family might have blocked us from being able to manifest a healthy and fulfilling life. It is important for us to acknowledge the hurts, betrayals, and traumas that occurred in our childhood. At the same time it is important to remember that you would not be here if you were not carrying gifts and strengths through your ancestral line.

It is empowering and healing to explore and honor your ancestry. Your ancestors are supporting you. They do want to see you be healthy, happy, and successful. Like your helping spirits, your ancestors lend invisible spiritual support to guide you through your life. Most of us are simply not aware of the invisible support we receive from our ancestors. However, I do hear people share how an ancestor might appear in a dream and offer support and guidance. But most do not have a regular practice of connecting with and honoring the ancestral spirits who deeply care about our well-being.

To connect with your ancestors, who might also be helping spirits for you, brings a richness into your life, for it connects you to your ancestral line and provides you with rich stories and a sense of your personal history. At the same time some people who have been abused by a family member might not feel ready for this work. Once ready, this work can be a true source of healing as old hurtful memories are replaced with stories of love and support.

When Karen performed a journey to her mother's line, she was shown that she was carrying through a wealth of knowledge of how to use her intuition. Lori watched her father's family in past history perform shamanic dances and ceremonies. Michael was able to meet his ancestors that he knew nothing about as he was given up at birth for adoption. Being able to learn about his birth family was a source of great healing.

If you feel ready for an exploration into your ancestral line, here is a journey you can perform. You can perform a series of journeys to continue to gain more knowledge from your helping ancestors.

JOURNEY TO YOUR MOTHER'S AND FATHER'S LINEAGES

The first intention for this journey is to be shown your mother's line. Next, you will ask to learn about your father's line and what you are carrying through from these ancestors.

It is a healing journey to be able to go back and explore the gifts, talents, and strengths that you inherited. But this is not all, as you want to establish a relationship with your ancestral spirits and continue to learn from them. Ask to meet your ancestors in either the Lower World or Upper World and start to converse with them. Let them share their stories with you. Tell them your dreams and tell them what you want. Learn how they provide you with invisible spiritual support. You might receive a message from your ancestors, or you might receive a transmission of energy.

Once you have learned what you can for now, give thanks to your ancestors, and return from this journey.

You might need to repeat a series of journeys to gain the information you are seeking. Once you have learned some stories about your ancestors, there is another journey you can take to experience the ancestral energy that supports you.

JOURNEY TO YOUR ANCESTRAL LINE

The intention for this journey is to experience the pure energy that you are carrying through your ancestral line. In this way you are going beyond the story and allowing yourself to feel the spiritual force of support behind you.

It does not matter who your ancestors were and what they did. They were part of this Earth and carried to you a richness of knowledge of how to live. Experiencing this energy will help you to feel a deep power growing in the soil of your inner landscape. You will feel a deeper sense of being rooted to the earth.

Return feeling revitalized and connected to your ancestral line. Notice the flow of energy you now feel in your body.

4

Nature Is Our Greatest Healer and a Spiritual Ally

THIS PART OF THE BOOK began by offering journeys that introduce you to your power animal or guardian spirit, and your teacher. This is because they are essential guides into the hidden realms who can accompany you in all aspects of your shamanic life. But on the most basic level, shamanism is about relating with nature.

Nature is a doorway into perceiving the world we live in a new and fresh way. Nature helps to awaken us out of the collective trance and helps us to remember how we are connected to all that is alive. Spend time in nature and recognize the divinity in the trees, plants, rocks, animals, birds, insects, and elements. See your reflection in everything that is alive. Mother Theresa taught, "If you look at a rock, you will see your reflection." Spending time in nature improves your health and level of happiness. It teaches us how to cooperate with change versus resisting change.

Focusing on a positive vision while surrendering the outcome is a paradox we all must learn to hold while doing our spiritual work. A powerful way to learn how to cooperate with change and to dance this paradox is by spending time in nature. The cycles of nature and the changing seasons teach us about important principles of life such as birth, growth, regeneration, flow, rest, letting go, death, and evolution. We understand that death and birth are all cycles of life and that everything in nature is part of the process of evolution. Change happens in nature all the time. By spending time in nature, we learn how to engage more fully in life.

As I have shared, from a shamanic point of view, everything that exists is alive. Trees, plants, animals, reptiles, insects, rocks, and so on are alive, and all have a spirit. The same teachings in nature that informed the ancients are the same teachings that inform us today.

JOURNEYING TO VISIT WITH NATURE BEINGS

Having a continual practice where you journey to the different spirits of nature is really important. You can perform a Middle World journey to learn from the trees, plants, rocks, minerals, and animal life where you live. I mentioned a powerful journey I had years ago. In the journey I was exploring the original roots of shamanism. As I shared in chapter 1, I had a vivid experience of being shown how plants taught the people the shamanic practices needed to heal and to live a healthy way of life.

Journey in the Middle World to meet the plants, trees, rocks, minerals, and other nature beings where you live. You will connect with a variety of nature beings who will introduce themselves as allies that you can add to your community of invisible helpers.

JOURNEY TO THE MIDDLE WORLD
TO LEARN FROM NATURE BEINGS

The entrance to your house or the building where you are journeying is the doorway into the Middle World. While you drum, rattle, or listen to a track of shamanic music, experience yourself walking outside your door. In your journey visit with a plant, tree, rock, or nature being that you have seen in ordinary reality. By journeying, you will find you can communicate with this nature being to establish a relationship with it and learn about its nature. Open all of your senses in the journey. You might get a sense of a message in your body, hear an auditory message, or see a symbol in your mind's eye when you communicate with this nature spirit.

When you return, reflect on how you can deepen your relationship with the nature being in your area.

LISTENING TO OUR SHARED WISDOM

Spending time out in nature is the *best* way to learn about nature. The more time we can spend in nature, the healthier we become. It is important for our health and well-being to feel fully nourished by the beauty of life. Spending time in nature provides such nourishment. No healing method replaces putting your feet on or lying on the earth, absorbing the power of the sun, seeing the beauty of the sky, and reveling in the awesome light of the stars and moon. Nature is our greatest healer.

Connecting to nature has always been an essential and core teaching in shamanic cultures. And now with all the dramatic shifts that are occurring through climate change, it is important to learn how to harmonize with nature. On a spiritual level the extreme changes in the climate are mirroring back to us the imbalance of how we live. The Salish people of the northwest use the word *skalatitude.* This is a powerful word that means when people and nature are in perfect harmony, then magic and beauty are everywhere. This goes back to the principle of reciprocity. As we honor nature, nature honors us.

I live a few miles outside of downtown Santa Fe. There is an *arroyo,* a dry riverbed, below my house that runs for miles in two directions. In Santa Fe County it is illegal to fence off your property, so people can walk or ride horses through the entire length of the arroyo. Although there are many houses where I live, when you enter into the arroyo and walk through the dry riverbed, you cannot see them. It is such a gift to live in a place where I can easily enter nature and be completely unaware of the population that surrounds me.

I have been walking through this arroyo for the twenty years I have lived in my home. Sometimes I jog through the arroyo simply for exercise and allow my mind to wander. And there are times when I walk slowly, deeply connecting with the wealth of plants and trees that grow here. Surrounding the arroyo are juniper, pinion pine, ponderosa, cottonwood, and aspen trees. I have gotten to know many of these trees, and over the years I have felt that I have connected so deeply with some of them that I can truly call them my friends. Sometimes even when the air is still as I approach certain trees, the leaves rustle as if greeting me.

There is one ancient ponderosa pine tree that is so magnificent and seems to thrive during the most extreme climate changes such as cold, heat, wind, and drought. There is even a bench with cushions on it reserved for the elderly. This tree gets a great deal of love and respect from the local residents. Some trees I worry about. I can watch them struggling. I do my work to not project struggle and illness onto them. I see them in their divine light, and I often touch the trunk and deeply feel the bark of the tree and radiate love and light. And there are times when I walk through the arroyo in a very focused state and perceive all the trees in their divine light as I walk.

There are also times when I do not feel well emotionally or physically and ask that the trees recognize me in my divinity. Nature is intelligent and does recognize you. As you look at nature, nature is also looking at you.

Allow nature to inspire and take you into a deeper place within, where you can be informed by your inner spirit. Sitting by running water, such as a river, stream, or waterfall, can help you be transported away from the ordinary world where your inner wisdom can rise up. Watching waves in the ocean creates a state of opening so that you can listen to the messages of your soul. Finding a place on the Earth where you can look out into the distance can be comforting as your daily thoughts simply dissolve.

During such quiet time, you can hear your inner voice sharing guidance with you. Sitting in the breezes or the winds and just listening allows your ordinary thoughts to fly away and be replaced by your inner voice providing guidance for you in your life. Let the wind play with your hair as it unburdens you of any concerns. Building a campfire and gazing into the fire is a traditional way of moving into a shamanic trance where you can receive inspiration. Watching the flame of a candle can do the same.

When we take a walk in nature and speak to the spirit of the elements and to other nature beings, true wisdom comes to us through a transmission rather than a rational understanding. This energetic transmission touches a knowing that we are born with that acts as fertilizer for our growth.

HONORING NATURE BY FIRST GIVING THANKS

As you experienced when you did the guided meditation that opened this part of the book, before doing any ceremony or journeying to connect with the compassionate spirits and allies for guidance or healing, shamans acknowledge, thank, and welcome them. To keep balance in the web of life, people living in shamanic cultures have daily practices to honor the elements and all living beings. It is through honor, respect, and gratitude that balance is kept on the planet.

The helping spirits are always with you. But it is important to give thanks and simply acknowledge the help you will receive and honor your connections in the spirit world. This is simple courtesy. There are many helping spirits that shamans acknowledge before beginning their work. Over time you will feel called to give thanks and acknowledge the different helping spirits you work with time and time again.

You will feel inspired as you continue your shamanic practice to find your own way to welcome and acknowledge the spirits. Many shamans use rattling and whistling to do this. You can find an instrument that you might like to use. Or you can do a meditation in silence. The spirits read your heart not your mind. It is not the words that are most important. What is important is the intention behind your words. They experience the love and honor that you share with them. Your beginning ceremony will increase in power and meaning once you get your personal insights about the directions and helping spirits you wish to honor.

For now you can use the meditation that I shared to begin this part of the book to greet, acknowledge, and honor the directions and the helping spirits.

GETTING TO KNOW THE SEVEN DIRECTIONS

The seven directions—East, South, West, North, the Sky above, the Earth below, and the Spirit within you—have particular meanings in different shamanic cultures. In some cultures shamans start by honoring the East and some the South. The colors and the elements—earth, air, water, and fire—associated with directions vary from culture to culture. Some shamanic cultures work with six directions while some include the Spirit Within. And in some shamanic cultures, space (within and without) is honored as a direction. There is no *one way* to work with the directions

As you proceed with your work and also spend time in nature, the directions might take on a particular meaning that touches you personally, and you might find yourself sinking into qualities that you feel represent them. Beholding landmarks such as the mountains or the ocean, watching the rising and setting sun, and observing how weather comes in will inspire associations for you. You can learn more about the meaning of the directions by journeying to them.

THE ELEMENTS INFORM, BALANCE, AND HEAL

The elements of earth, air, water, and fire are living beings too. It is important for us to learn how to reconnect with the elements, because we *are* earth, air, water, and fire. Living a life of honor and respect toward the elements creates a harmonious life because the principle of reciprocity in shamanism is key. When we respect nature, then nature will respect us. Gratitude kindles your connection to the elements. Once we give gratitude to the elements, then nature will honor and show respect to humankind.

During this time of increasing climate change, it is important for you to learn how to connect with the elements, which give you life. Air is a living being. Air welcomed you into your life with your very first breath. Air is the very last living being that you will say good-bye to as you leave this life with your last breath.

Water held you while you were in your mother's womb. Water escorted you into this world. It continues to nurture you as you drink and absorb the water needed to sustain you. Water also nurtures you through its beauty; it reflects back the beauty of your soul.

The earth shares an abundance of all you need to thrive. It reflects back your own beauty through other forms of life that are born, grow, and live on the earth. The wealth of colors and unique life forms delight you. You are nurtured and given life by all the food the earth so generously gives.

Fire as the sun is a teacher about unconditional giving. There is no life on this earth without sunlight. All life grows toward the sun. The sun continually emanates the light and energy you need to thrive. The sun and fire reflect back to your passion for life. Fire burns with great passion and helps you to remember the truth of who you are, which is light.

There are a variety of ways to connect spiritually with the elements. A potent way of working is to merge with an element while you are journeying. You can merge with your favorite element that you feel is an ally for you. I find one way to heal a fear about an element is to merge with that element. For example, Larry lost his house during a fire. He performed a merging journey with fire to learn about its behavior. Larry learned about the transformative power of fire, and when he became fire, he could understand how fire moves across the land to heal and to help the earth regenerate. Through this journey Larry was able to heal his troubled relationship with fire.

As you will experience in the journey that follows, to do this you journey in the Middle World. As I shared earlier in this chapter, in a Middle World journey the house or building you are in becomes your starting point.

The teachings we receive through merging journeys go beyond mental concepts and rational understanding, and impact us physically as we become one with the energy of another spiritual being.

JOURNEY TO THE MIDDLE WORLD
TO MERGE WITH AN ELEMENT

To perform a merging journey, set the intention by choosing which element you wish to merge with. Begin your journey experience in the Middle World by walking out of the house or building you are in. Walk into nature and find an element you wish to merge with. In this journey you learn about an element not by observing it but by becoming it. As you become an element, you learn about its nature. Once merged, feel the sensations of being this element.

If you would like to merge with air, set your intention that you want to become a gentle breeze or a strong wind blowing. Feel yourself blowing through the trees.

In merging with water, you might merge with a teardrop running down your cheek. You can merge with the mighty ocean, a stream or a raging river, a gentle drizzle, mist, or a torrential rain. Experience yourself as the ocean welling or flowing as a river.

You can merge with earth where you live. Feel yourself as solid, moist, cool earth. This journey will teach you a lot about your inner and outer landscape during seasonal changes.

You can journey to merge with fire by becoming the flame in a candle, a campfire, or a raging forest fire. Experience yourself as fire rising up and greeting the air.

When you hear the return beat, with intention, disconnect from the element and, with discipline, return back into the room that you are in.

You might find that an element volunteers itself as an ally and helping spirit for you. The element might share with you the strengths you need in your life that it can help you access.

Diane always had an issue with the wind. The winds were very fierce where she grew up, and as a child she felt completely out of control as she walked through the blowing wind. As she started performing merging journeys with air, she found that wind became her ally and taught her how to surrender and let go of control. Once she embraced the teaching, she went on to work with fire as an ally. As in Diane's case, you will find that there are elements you need to establish deeper relationships with.

Performing merging journeys over time is a way to do this. You can merge with earth where you live during the change of each season. This experience will show you what your own body experiences during winter, spring, summer, and fall.

Through experience I have found that merging with water tends to calm people and instill a sense of inner peace. People return fresh and regenerated. I recommend merging with water to students and clients who need to calm down.

Another series of journeys that you can work with involves merging with the elements within you, for you are earth, air, water, and fire. Merging with the fire within is very educational. Some people who suffer from anxiety notice that their fire is burning too strong, and they need to learn how to manage it. Fire can teach how to manage the flames. And for some people, their fire is not burning strong enough, creating depressive states. In this case fire can be a teacher of how to fuel and stoke one's internal fire to create passion.

Notice and get a sense for how all healthy elements are moving. If you merge with frozen earth, you will experience a lot of movement in the molecules. I have merged with ice, and I am in complete awe of how much movement there is.

When an element within becomes stagnant, illness can set in. You want to find ways to strengthen your body by incorporating physical exercise into your life to create a moving flow of energy. In lieu of merging with an element during a shamanic journey, you can walk in nature in a Middle World journey and visit an element you wish to learn from and connect with. You could visit a body of water and have a conversation with water. You might sit at a campfire and talk to fire. You can visit a sacred place on the earth and speak to earth. Air might share messages with you as you sit listening to the breezes.

NATURE PROVIDES YOU WITH SIGNPOSTS

As shamanism is a practice of direct revelation, don't limit yourself to having to perform a formal journey to receive guidance. You might find that you receive powerful guidance while taking a walk in nature while holding any stated intention, including those given for journeys in this book. You will naturally learn how the helping spirits share messages by showing us omens in nature. It is exciting to take walks and open to how much support and guidance the universe is giving you through showing you signs. Nature is a helping spirit for you, and as you deepen your connection with the natural world, you will find that nature shows you omens and signposts to light your way. Every place in nature provides a doorway connecting the visible and the invisible.

When I walk through the arroyo with questions or concerns, I find that nature continues to show me omens. I love working with omens, as this is a way to experience just how much support we are always being given by the universe. The universe, the helping spirits, and nature itself are always giving us signposts that light our path in life.

There are times that I have walked through my arroyo praying and crying, asking for some help to guide me through particularly challenging times. And I always receive an extraordinary sign showing that the universe is listening and sending help my way. There were two times when I received such extraordinary omens that I want to share with you.

Many years ago I was having a challenging time with someone whom I was connected with in my spiritual community. I had been walking on my treadmill focusing on this challenge. I heard a very clear message telling me to go walk in the arroyo and I would receive an omen. So I stopped my treadmill, put on a different pair of shoes for walking in sand, and began my walk. After walking for about ten minutes, a hawk came flying through the trees and right up to me and slapped my head with his wing. Then right behind him a hummingbird was flying and swooped down and slapped my head with his wing. My heart was beating so rapidly as I was shocked by being slapped across the head by the wings of both a hawk and a hummingbird. Then they both landed on a branch and sat right next to each other just staring at me for what felt like an eternity. No one moved. After a few minutes I finally continued walking. Can you imagine a hawk and a hummingbird sitting on a branch quietly next to each other and not moving? It was amazing. It took me quite awhile to get the message being shared. It is not always a simple matter to interpret signs and omens. But over time I got the message. From time to time I find myself thinking about this walk, as the hawk and hummingbird showing up was beyond the ordinary.

Another important message came to me a few years ago when I was really challenged with the care of my father at the end of his life. I had to make decisions that I felt were beyond what I was emotionally capable of. Hospice could support me on some levels, but they could not make certain decisions I was facing. One day I went into the arroyo. I was crying and praying for some help and a sign.

The day I went into the arroyo was a cold and rainy October day. As I was walking back home, a baby snake crawled over one of my shoes. I could not believe what I was seeing. As I was so distraught at the time, I was not thinking clearly. I bent down to see if it was a worm or some other nature being. It was a snake. October is certainly not a time for snakes to hatch. And a snake would not be out on a cold and rainy day. But there it was. I could not deny its appearance.

The omen to me meant that something was changing and transforming. I interpreted Snake as a sign of death and rebirth. And indeed my father did die shortly after I saw this omen. He ended up dying in a state of peace and grace. There was a new birth and a transition for my entire family. A snake will frequently appear during my walks when I need a sign that I am not alone, that I am held in the loving arms of the universe, and that the challenge I am facing will pass.

As I reflect on how many gifts I have received from walking in my arroyo, I feel strongly that it has been my regular ongoing relationship with the spirit of this place that has brought forth a wealth of signs to help me on my life journey. I not only walk the same path on a regular basis, but I also always walk with love, honor, and respect for all that is alive in this area. I believe it is the relationship I have built up with the nature beings here that has created such a deep and strong field that lifts the veils between the worlds. The help of the hidden realms can reach through to give me guidance and to let me know how much I am loved and supported.

NATURE LIVES WHEREVER YOU ARE

I did not always live in a place where I had the opportunity to go right outside my door and walk for miles in nature. I grew up in Brooklyn, and I sang to a tree outside my house every day. I spoke with it daily. I felt a wonderful reciprocal friendship with this tree. I also lived in San Francisco where I had my favorite walking paths in parks. I built up such a strong relationship with the nature beings there that I felt a strong sense of mutual love and support.

You can build up a mutually supportive relationship with nature wherever you live—in a city or in a rural environment. You can be nourished by nature where you live, although you might need to work a little harder at it due to the bricks and cement in the city. You can always touch a tree or a plant that is growing in your neighborhood. There might be a tree or plant you can radiate love to everyday. There are local parks you can walk in. There is the sky above and the earth below that you can continue to honor. You can honor the living beings we call earth, air, water, and the sun as you go about your day. It does not matter where you live; nature will respond to you, and your life will change. Your relationship with the universe will change as you notice signs being given to you to light your path and let you know you are being recognized, supported, and loved by the spirit that lives in all things. Most importantly, your deep connection with nature will fill your soul.

Hawk, Snake, Bear, Fox, Butterfly, and Dragonfly often visit me on my walks in my arroyo and also while I am walking in other places in nature when the universe is trying to give me a sign. The wind gives me some potent messages, and I have come to rely on the messages that travel through the wind and breezes when I need guidance. The more you work with enlivening your senses, you will be more aware of the omens and signs being shown to you. Notice who visits you.

As you hold questions about what is happening in your life, if you pay attention, the universe is always giving you a sign. In shamanic traditions these signs are called omens. By spending time in nature, you will learn how the spirits call to you. Here are some examples of how they communicate:

As you walk to work, you might see the appearance of an animal whose qualities provide an answer to your question.

You might notice forms appearing in the clouds presenting a metaphorical answer to your question.

Sometimes you will see a poster of your power animal on the side of a bus or on the wall of building just when you really need to feel supported by the universe.

You might look down while walking and notice that there is a heart-shaped rock that might serve as a sign and a gift for you.

A stranger might appear and during a casual conversation says the perfect words or phrases that provide insight into a question or challenge you have been pondering.

Omens are shown in surprising and unexpected ways. You need to learn how to be observant. In native cultures people walk in nature and listen with their whole body. This means they fully open their senses to everything in their environment. Find a park or a place in nature, and connect with nature everyday. As you build up a relationship, notice how the universe responds to your questions, challenges, and prayers.

LEAVING OFFERINGS AS GIFTS OF LOVE AND APPRECIATION

Oftentimes I leave offerings for the land and helping spirits during a walk. Leaving offerings is a way of thanking the Spirit of the Land and the nature beings for connecting with us. Corn is a sacred plant to the native people of the Southwest. It is food and is the symbol of life itself. I leave cornmeal to give thanks to the land and helping spirits. Blue is my favorite color, so I gift the land with blue corn meal. I also leave lavender that was grown in my garden as an offering.

You can journey on a sacred plant or herb, or even food that you might like to leave in thanks for all you receive from the nature spirits. Offer gifts to the land, water, and trees, and offer other nature beings a gift of herbs or food. Even if you live in a city, there are still trees and the elements of earth, air, water, and the sun that you can thank. As you leave your offerings, talk to the nature beings and deepen your relationship with them. Do remember that animals and birds will eat your offerings. Please consider only leaving offerings that are safe for them to eat.

One way for me to offer my heartfelt gratitude to the Earth is to write the word *LOVE* in the ground after a new snow or in the moist ground after a rain. It not only feels good to make an offering of love, but you will feel more connected to the Earth and all of nature.

LEARNING HOW THE CYCLES OF SUN AND MOON AFFECT YOU

We rely so heavily on modern technology, leading to a false perception that we are separate from nature. Separating ourselves and disconnecting from nature and its cycles has created a tremendous amount of emotional and physical illness. We are part of the cycles of nature. Learning how to personally connect with the cycles of nature will impact your emotional and physical health in a positive way. When you walk against the river of life, you start to feel worn down. Part of creating inner transformation and leading the life you want to live is learning how to live in harmony with nature's cycles.

We watch the moon and its cycles creating rising and receding tides of the ocean. The seasons affect all of life, and we do flow with them, whether we are conscious of it or not. We know there are times to rest and times to be more active. The shining stars above us act as guides in our life and reflect back to us the light shining within. When we align our life with the stars, we find that life flows easier.

You are nature. You are part of nature's cycles, and you must learn how to realign your personal cycle with the cycle of the changing seasons and with the lunar cycles. The cycles of the moon affect water. As you are mostly water, the moon affects you too. Instead of walking *against* the river of life, you need to learn how to walk *with* the river of life. We are unique and feel different inner energetic shifts as the moon cycles and the seasons change. For example:

Some people have more energy and are more extroverted during the full moon while others might feel introverted and drawn within.

Some people feel more energetic, healthier, more vital, and more social at the new moon again while others might feel the need for alone time and silence.

Some people feel like they want to be engaged in outer activities in the spring and summer.

There are people that just *love* the fall and winter and wake up and feel more alive during these seasons.

A good way to start this work is to observe over time how your energy shifts and how you feel during different seasons and lunar cycles.

Create a journal and take notes describing how you feel at different phases of the moon and seasonal changes.

I leave offerings as a gift to the land at each solstice and equinox. This is a way to welcome in each new season by performing a simple ceremony of gratitude. You can leave an offering of gratitude for all the helping spirits and spiritual allies who provide guidance and healing in your life. Performing such a simple ceremony helps you to acknowledge the change occurring in the Earth and in your body as you begin a new cycle.

You can also journey to learn more about these relationships. Journey to the moon to learn more about how you can harmonize with the cycles within and without. This was an important journey for me to take when learning how I could make changes to schedule my life so that I was honoring my inner cycle to harmonize with the moon. When I journeyed to the moon, she showed me through movement how my cycle aligns with hers. I was able to get a direct experience of the changing feeling in my body as she danced her cycle for me. There are stories about the moon that come from different shamanic cultures. Some cultures perceive the moon as male and some as female. Go with your direct experience.

JOURNEY TO THE MOON AND HER CYCLES

Set your intention to journey to the moon. You do not need the assistance of a helping spirit to take you to the moon. But if you would like a helping spirit to accompany you, call your spirit to you before undertaking this journey.

Journey to the moon and learn from this spiritual ally. You can dance the cycles, noticing how the phases impact your movement. Learn about the energy and power of its cycles beyond what you might already know. Ask the moon what changes you need to make in how you schedule your life so that you can harmonize with her cycles.

Once you feel complete with your journey, return to the room you are in.

5

Your Invisible *and* Visible Shamanic Community

WHEN I FIRST MOVED TO SANTA FE, I found that I was out of alignment with the energy here. I could not move my life in a positive direction. I kept hearing about the magic of Santa Fe, but this description did not match my experience at all. I had a very strong journey practice and was teaching shamanism to others. To cure the misalignment that I felt, I decided to use journeying as a tool to explore what my issue was and how to change the course of my life.

I decided to journey to the Spirit of Santa Fe. I wanted to find out why my life was so disharmonious here and filled with pain and suffering. I set an intention to ask for guidance on what changes I needed to make to move my life in a positive direction. The Spirit of Santa Fe appeared to me as a beautiful woman with long flowing golden hair and intense blue eyes. As the spirits are formless, they change their form as they appear to different people. Therefore, someone else journeying to the Spirit of Santa Fe might be met by a form with a different physical description.

The Spirit of Santa Fe showed me compassion, but she exhibited very tough love toward me. I have found this to be true of most of my non-ordinary teachers. The teachers I work with do not show sympathy toward me as I go through challenges. Instead they ask me to stand up and find the inner strength within to move forward.

First the Spirit of Santa Fe shared with me how I was out of alignment with her energy. Next she gave me five tasks to do. I followed her advice and completed each of the five tasks. Since that time my life here shifted 180 degrees. I went from believing that life here was filled with misery to experiencing the magic of Santa Fe.

The Spirit of Santa Fe remained my teacher for many years. One day in a journey she told me she had taught me what I needed to learn from her. She said that I could now leave Santa Fe if I wanted to. It was clear to me that Santa Fe was a place I needed to be for a while for my personal growth and evolution. The Spirit of Santa Fe assured me that if I wanted to continue living here, it would always be my home. Santa Fe has been my home for thirty years, and I have no desire to leave.

The land and city where you live is alive. It has a spirit, and you can learn so much from connecting to the spirit. You can learn how to live a life filled with harmony, how to live a healthy life, and also how to move into alignment with the spirit of the land. By connecting to the spirit of the land, you will become a better caretaker of your inner and outer garden.

JOURNEY TO THE SPIRIT OF THE LAND WHERE YOU LIVE

After completing your preparation work, set your intention to meet the Spirit of the Land you live on and the Spirit of the City. It does not matter if you live in an urban environment. Each city has a spirit. Under the concrete is a powerful spiritual life force.

Meet the spirit of where you live, and ask for suggestions on how to work and live in a harmonious way. Also ask for advice on how to create a state of health and positive transformation in your life. You might ask how to move your life into alignment with the Spirit of the Land. Ask for suggestions on how you can manifest and attract to yourself meaningful work or a love relationship if you are looking for one. Ask how you can meet with others in your community who are also in alignment with the spirit of where you live.

When you return from this journey, reflect on how you can put into action the advice and suggestions you received.

When shamans traveled to work in places outside of their home, they always asked permission of the local spirits to enter the landscape and to do their work. I have noticed such a difference in my travels when I began carrying on this tradition. I journey to the spirit of every city I travel to so the Spirit of the City knows I am coming. When teaching I talk to the Spirit of the Land about the goodhearted participants who are traveling to the workshop. I give thanks to the spirit for welcoming me and the participants in the training. I give thanks to them for creating a beautiful sacred space for us to connect, heal, grow, and evolve together.

Before greeting friends and others when you travel, start by greeting the Spirit of the Land. You will experience the land reaching up to touch your feet with love as it greets you.

THE HIDDEN FOLK JOIN YOU IN BEING A CARETAKER OF THE EARTH

As you connect with the Spirit of the Land it is also important to reconnect with the Middle World nature spirits. Indigenous cultures recognize that there are forms of nature spirits that were once visible to us as children. As adults most of us cut off our connections with these beings. We call these nature spirits such names as fairies, devas, elves, forest guardians, and forest angels. Some people refer to them as the little people. As these beings can be taller than humans, I call them the Hidden Folk.

The Hidden Folk appear in stories, myths, and legends, written by people all over the world. Just like us, they are caretakers of this great Earth. By calling in and working in partnership with these beings, we can heal our planet. In the 1960s a spiritual community formed in Findhorn, Scotland. The soil was sand, and the conditions were simply not right for growing food. But this community wanted to create gardens where they could grow food. They could have thought this is impossible and that the land was not fertile enough to grow food.

They ended up having the opportunity to work in partnership with nature spirits and spiritual beings in the Middle World who helped them to grow an amazing wealth of vegetables. They grew vegetables that were larger than any of us would believe possible. People traveled from around the world to witness these miraculous gardens. Another example is Perelandra, started in Virginia by Machaelle Small Wright, where miraculous gardens are grown by collaborating with the nature spirits. At Perelandra there is a strong working partnership with the Hidden Folk to grow healthy fruits and vegetables.

As children we knew the Hidden Folk, and they brought a sense of magic and joy into our lives. Opening the veils to meet the Hidden Folk returns light and a twinkle to our eyes. The key is to work with the nature spirits in partnership. The Hidden Folk remain elusive until they feel they can trust humans in being committed to caretake the Earth. They will not do the work for us. But they will work with us.

Whether you live in a city or in the country, there are Hidden Folk where you live. It is time to meet them and find out just how you can work in partnership with them to caretake the Earth. The Hidden Folk are members of your invisible community of helping spirits.

JOURNEY TO MEET THE HIDDEN FOLK WHERE YOU LIVE

Meeting the Hidden Folk where you live can be done through a shamanic journey. Or you can find a place outdoors where you can sit in meditation and call to them. You will sense them. But you might have an easier time by visiting them in the invisible realm of the Middle World.

In your journey, walk outside and experience yourself connecting first with the Spirit of the Land. Then call to the Hidden Folk—introduce yourself to the nature beings that show up. They can take a variety of forms from small fairies and beings of the *devic* realms to immense forest guardians and angels. Let these nature spirits know that you live your life from a place of heart and that you love all of life and the Earth.

The Hidden Folk are not always trusting of humans as we have destroyed so much of nature and have not been honoring the environment. Ask the Hidden Folk how you can partner with them to caretake the land where you live. Be aware that if you do choose to ask them this question, they will give you tasks. They are not satisfied with working with people who want them to do all the work.

You can also ask them what kind of offerings they would like you to leave for them on the land—any drinks or food that they like. The Hidden Folk appreciate when you leave offerings for them as a way of honoring them.

When you are done with your journey, return with a new sense of belonging to a larger spiritual community in all worlds.

A student of mine named Michelle was sad about leaving a workshop. She had developed such a deep friendship with others in the group. Michelle recently had recovered from a serious illness and found wonderful support in working with a loving and supportive community. When we were at our ending lunch together, she started crying.

I sat with her and asked her why she was feeling so sad. She told me she did not want to go home where she would lose the physical sense of being with loving people. Michelle was afraid of returning to a lonely life. I instructed her to send out a message to the Hidden Folk where she lived. She was to ask them to welcome her home and surround her with love and support.

When Michelle went home nothing in the ordinary or physical realm had changed. But she felt a sparkle in her house she had not experienced before. She could feel the presence of loving and compassionate spirits. Michelle told me that she no longer felt alone.

Elaine shared with me that after meeting both the Spirit of the Land and the Hidden Folk when she returned home from a workshop, she noticed a difference. She could feel the land and the nature beings welcoming her home. Her relationship with the land deepened. Her garden began to flourish. She felt a joyful connection with the land that she had not experienced before.

Journeying to the Spirit of the Land and the Hidden Folk will assist you in establishing a relationship with the spirit of nature where you live. You will notice a change in your relationship with the land or the city that is your home. As the Hidden Folk observe how you behave toward nature and honor the web of life, they will trust you more. Once they trust you, they will share information with you that will be quite deep and meaningful about how to live a harmonious and joy-filled life.

GATHERING OTHER PEOPLE
IN YOUR COMMUNITY

In the practice of shamanic healing it is well understood that there is an exponential power when we work in community versus when we work alone. Someone who is ill might approach a group of people in a shamanic community. It is amazing to track the difference of the results when somebody works privately with one practitioner versus when a community works together in behalf of an individual. The same would be true in gathering the spiritual energy of a group to work in behalf of a community or the planet.

I am inspired as I watch the news and see how people are coming together in community to support each other. After a climatic event such as a tornado, typhoon, hurricane, or earthquake people in communities are gathering together to help each other rebuild their homes and their lives. People in inner cities are joining together in community to plant community gardens. People in local communities welcome home the men and women who served in the military, letting them know how much their efforts and actions are appreciated. It does not matter whether or not you support war. Veterans deserve to be welcomed home.

We can add to the power of what is being done in the ordinary realms with our spiritual work. When we join our hearts together as a supportive community, we have great potential to transform individuals, local communities, and the planet.

CREATING A PRAYER TREE

Here is a wonderful tradition you can share to bring your community together. You can create a prayer tree for loved ones, coworkers, and community to tie prayer ribbons on the branches to support each other's prayers. It is something that you can create in your house, at work, and in your community. This tradition is seen in many different countries. I first learned about it as a Siberian tradition, where it is common to find a prayer tree. In Siberia trees are seen as the most sacred beings because they bridge heaven and earth. They bridge heaven through their branches and the earth through their roots. As humans we bridge heaven and earth with our arms up to heaven and our feet planted on the earth. We create that bridge through our hearts.

Juniper trees are typically used for a Siberian prayer tree. The shaman divines the appropriate tree. After the right tree is found, there are days of ceremony performed where traditional food and drink offerings are left by the tree. The tree is honored for volunteering to carry prayers to the creative forces of the universe. The shaman in the community chants and gives thanks to the helping spirits for carrying the prayers of the people up to the universe so that their dreams can manifest on Earth. The ribbons tied on to the tree are empowered by individuals in the community with personal prayers for themselves, for loved ones, for family, and the community.

You can see these trees throughout Siberia with brightly colored large ribbons tied on branches. I saw a photo of a prayer tree in Siberia where there were so many ribbons and pieces of fabric on the tree, the branches started touching the ground. The branches had become so heavy from all the ribbons empowered with the prayers of those who made pilgrimages to the tree. An important teaching is to tie the ribbons loosely onto the branches so their growth is not choked off or stunted.

Since I started teaching how to create a prayer tree, people from many parts of Europe and even Turkey shared stories with me about ancient traditions of prayer trees, wishing trees, and blessing trees. Simin Uysal is a brilliant shamanic teacher in Turkey. She said, "Traveling in Anatolia, one can be surprised by the sudden appearance of a tree with pieces of fabric hanging from it. They are wishing trees where people typically tie pieces of fabric from personal items like scarves, handkerchiefs, or ribbons. Prayers are said silently while tying on the fabrics. You can sometimes see a person distributing offerings to others under the tree after their wish comes true. People make pilgrimages to them, walk around them, and make vows to them. These trees are not cut down and are protected by everyone. The wishing trees typically stand alone, either on a hilltop, in the middle of a vast plain, next to the tomb of a dervish or a water spring. The ones I have seen were beech, oak, mulberry, juniper, myrtle, cedar, and pine trees."[1]

While I was teaching in Scotland many years ago a friend took me to the Fairy Forest. It is a sacred place of prayer. People visit the trees here and tie ribbons on branches empowered with prayers. They leave letters written to God containing prayers. You see drawings, photos, gifts, food, and prayers for personal and planetary healing. It is quite the sight. I was very touched when I visited the Fairy Forest. I started to think about how many people decorate Christmas trees. What if we substituted the idea of Christmas trees and dedicated a tree where people could tie on prayers on the branches? I am not one who supports cutting down a tree simply to use as a decoration.

Find a tree in nature where people can make a pilgrimage to it to tie on prayer ribbons. Or you can bring a plant to your home or office. One way to work is to create a prayer bowl if you cannot find a tree, bush, or plant to use. This tree, bush, plant, or bowl would serve your community. Place it in your home or in the office where you work. You can invite people to tie on colored ribbons that contain prayers, either personal prayers or for loved ones, for the community, or for the planet. You can perform your own personal ceremony to give thanks to the plant or the tree and leave offerings. You can encourage people to use some form of craft, such as knitting, crocheting, carving, to make an offering that can be left at the prayer tree, imbuing and holding the power of their prayers. People can write down wishes and prayers on a piece of paper to leave in a bowl dedicated to receiving prayers. It's a great way to bring coworkers and others in your community together to support the prayers of each other. Use your imagination, remember, the key is the intention and the love that you put into creating this ceremony.

The times we live in call us to strengthen our local communities. In shamanic cultures the strength of the community was dependent on each member contributing his or her inherent gifts to the health of the community at large. It is time to trust our gifts, knowledge, and wisdom and share our strength and tools with others.

PART 3

Evoking Transformation

Close your eyes and take some deep cleansing breaths. Let go of the concerns and events of your day. Feel your feet on the floor, connecting deeply with the Earth. Feel the Earth greeting you and embracing you with love. Experience the sensation of connection through your feet. As you feel your connection with the Earth know that the Earth is sending you love. To receive the benefit of any healing, you must be able to absorb fully into your cells the love, light, and power of the Earth and the universe.

Think of a flowering plant that has been in the rain, and the sun finally shines through the clouds. The flower soaks in the light. Or imagine a dry sponge as it soaks in and absorbs water. Soak in and absorb the love and light of the Earth.

Take a few minutes for self-appreciation. You have been through many personal challenges that helped you to grow into the person you are today. Appreciate your persistence in moving through these challenges and how you did not let these challenges prevent you from moving forward to be sculpted into the beauty of who you are now.

You deserve to be whole, and you deserve to receive the healing needed for you to live a life filled with good health, joy, and love. Open up to the love of the Earth and the universe as you proceed to receive healing through the connection with your helping spirits.

6

Healing *for* Body, Mind, *and* Soul

IN TRADITIONAL CULTURES PEOPLE were raised from childhood learning how to live in harmony with others in their community and with nature. When an illness occurred, they knew what was causing it was a state of disharmony. In the Western world, the focus in our early education tends to be on academic subjects, how to be successful, and how to adapt and fit into society. Many of us did not learn the skill of self-reflection needed to truly understand how our way of life has led to certain illnesses and a general state of disharmony.

You can journey to your helping spirits for guidance and information, and you can also journey to them when you are in need of healing. The challenge you are facing might have manifested as an emotional or physical issue. In traditional cultures, people in need of healing sought out a shaman who could perform the necessary healing ceremony. Today many people make great progress asking for healing in their own journeys while others do need the healing help of a shamanic practitioner. Many people today misunderstand the healing work performed by shamans. There is a belief that shamanic healing is an active role for the shaman and totally passive for the client. During the healing ceremony, the role of the client might be a passive one. But the client has an active role in doing his or her personal work. In shamanic cultures it is understood that the strength of each person is needed to contribute to the health of the community. Each person knew the personal work needed to be done to return after healing from an illness as a vital community member.

In my experience as a shamanic practitioner, I perceive a clear distinction between *curing* and *healing*. If a *cure* is provided by a shamanic practitioner, by your helping spirits through a journey, or through a dream, it does not mean the work is done. If you have completed a lot of personal work to examine what changes need to be made in your life that will support long-term healing, then the *spiritual cure* might be the last step of the work. But if you have not done your personal work to examine how your lifestyle, your relationships, your work, and your disconnection with nature are feeding into your mental, emotional, and physical challenges, then the *spiritual cure* is the beginning of the work.

Shamanic *healing* does not involve a practitioner passing a magic wand over you. You do have to take responsibility in your own process of healing. Looking at some of the changes you need to make in life that lead to healing will be a focus of many of the exercises in *Walking in Light*.

Before you visit a helping spirit to ask for a healing, it is important that you understand that the effects vary. You might have a profound and immediate effect from such a journey. You might find that the journey needs to be repeated a few times. And you might find that the effects are very subtle until you do more personal work deepening the healing over time. There are times when you might be too close to your issue to be objective enough to discover during a journey an unidentified wound that needs healing. In this case you might ask a trained shamanic practitioner to journey on your behalf.

In shamanic healing work there's a difference between what you truly need versus what you think you need or want. Surrender to your helping spirits; let them assist you in the way that is best for your healing process. For this journey, you can make a decision to visit your power animal, guardian spirit, or teacher and ask for a healing. In future journeys you can request healing help from different helping spirits such as earth, air, water, fire, or another nature being such as the spirit of a plant, tree, or mineral.

JOURNEY TO ASK FOR HEALING

Journey to the Lower World or Upper World to meet a power animal, guardian spirit, or a teacher in human form and present an emotional or physical issue that you believe needs to be healed. You can state an issue you are dealing with, or you can say, "Please provide the healing that I need right now." You can also state a decree, "Thank you for performing a healing on my behalf." Whenever you state a decree as an intention, it acknowledges that the healing work you are requesting is already being done. Be clear on your intention as this will help you to have a focused journey.

This is a powerful journey that can create deep healing for you. Please honor the power of this journey by doing your preparation work to get into a spiritual state of consciousness.

Experience your starting place in nature, opening up all your invisible senses to be there now. Notice the landscape you are in, listen to the sounds of the elements, animal life, and other beings in nature. Breathe in the fragrances, feel the quality of the air and the earth beneath your feet. Whatever your unique style of journeying is, remember to trust and embrace your way of working.

When you feel ready, begin your journey to the Lower or Upper World and focus on your intention. You are requesting a healing. Surrender to the love and light of your helping spirits. Experience all that occurs.

Once you hear the return beat or when you feel complete, say thank you and good-bye to your helping spirit, and retrace your steps returning to the room you are in. Take a few minutes to rest and breathe, noticing how you are feeling. Feel your heart beating. Notice any changes of energy moving through your hands, feet, or other locations in your body. Are your fingers tingling? Notice if you are breathing easily and deeply. Is there a release of tension anywhere in your body? Reflect on what happened during this healing ceremony. After a few minutes you can take some notes, get up and walk around your room, or take a short walk outside. Notice if you are feeling different.

SPONTANEOUS HEALINGS

Sometimes the helping spirits will perform a spontaneous healing for you while you are journeying. You might be journeying on one intention, and during the journey your helping spirit bypasses your original intention to provide healing.

This happened to Susan. She was journeying to consult with her helping spirit about a challenge she was having at work. While on the journey her power animal surprised her by performing a soul retrieval for her, retrieving a part of herself that she lost at the time of a car accident. As this was an unexpected surprise, all her filters and emotional boundaries were down allowing her to truly soak in the light of the soul.

I love hearing the wealth of stories of helping spirits providing spontaneous healings. Students have reported such beautiful stories of their helping spirits removing blockages, performing soul retrievals, or filling them with light. Many of my students shared with me how a helping spirit performed a healing ceremony that did not have a particular form but left the person feeling revitalized and healed.

These spontaneous healings that occur in a journey are unexpected and are a gift. I believe it all has to do with right timing, meaning the helping spirits give us what we need when it is time, and when we are *ripe* for healing to occur.

OTHER DOORWAYS INTO HEALING

As I mentioned earlier, the helping spirits might role-play an issue that you need to look at. You can perform a journey and ask the spirits to show you an issue that needs healing in your life. For example, your helping spirit might show you that you have been betrayed earlier in life and that this betrayal is still impacting you as you try and create the life you wish to live. You can then ask for guidance on how to proceed with healing this issue. Your helping spirit might perform a healing ceremony to release this issue from your life. Or it might advise you on a series of ceremonies and healing practices you can do for yourself.

Another intention you can use for a journey is to ask your helping spirit, "What is the teaching I am receiving from the physical or emotional challenge I am facing? What are some ways to go about healing my issue?" During a time of depression in my life, my Upper World teacher Isis led me to the River of Grief in the Lower World. I was invited to bathe in the river as I was encouraged to cry and fully express my pain. This river is a place that exists in the invisible realms and is a profound place of healing. I have bathed in the River of Grief often. Some of my students share how they were taken to healing lakes or waterfalls. Some have been led into healing temples in the Upper World. I have led many of my students in workshops to a crystal healing cave in the Lower World. There are a wealth of locations in the non-ordinary realms your helping spirit can lead you to where you will find healing.

A helping spirit might brush your hair as it cleanses and releases negative energy from your energy field. Or a helping spirit might use tools such as a feather, a crystal, or smoke just as a shaman in the ordinary realm might use to heal you.

As I wrote in chapter 4, "Nature is Our Greatest Healer and a Spiritual Ally," I have collected many stories of people finding healing by spending time in nature and lying on the earth daily for fifteen minutes or more. There are so many different shamanic practices to explore when you are in need of healing.

Although there are classic diagnoses of illness as soul loss, a spiritual blockage, or a possessing spirit, there are unlimited ways of healing these issues. We often put healing in a box and believe that there is one method to go with each diagnosis. Shamans work with invisible and formless energies. When we give the issue over to the spirits, they know how to bring through the energies needed to transform the challenges we are facing.

You do not need to *beg* your helping spirit for its healing help; your helping spirit knows what you need. Surrender to its love and assistance. My suggestion is to hold an intention for healing in your daily life. Start each day by honoring and welcoming the spirits. State that you are open to healing and give thanks for the healing you are receiving now and will continue to receive with your spiritual work. Let go of the outcome and notice how healing happens in spontaneous and beautiful ways.

HEALING DREAMS

Besides using journeying, you might receive a healing during a dream. Some of the material I teach has come through my dreams. Over the years I have received numerous letters from people, most of whom I never met, sharing that I appeared to them in a dream to give them a message or to perform a healing. Dreams are a portal into the spiritual realms and dreaming is a shamanic practice. Some practitioners use dreaming as way to perform shamanic work.

I have found that dreams have been a very powerful way for me to receive healing. The healing that comes can be quite spontaneous. But you can also hold the intention and ask for a healing dream. You can also ask for a teaching before you go to sleep at night. In a dream you might receive guidance to help you work through a challenge or find solutions to issues you are facing.

In the early 1980s I suffered from a physical condition that was very painful. It was not a serious or critical illness that would affect the longevity of my life. But my physical problem affected the quality of my life, and I felt that I just could not bear to live life with this kind of chronic pain. Every night before I went to sleep I prayed for help to come through a dream. I was persistent. I didn't give up. I did not even know what a healing dream was. I was desperate, as I could not get any alleviation of my symptoms by working with the medical profession. I journeyed, endlessly asking for help. I asked friends to journey for me. Nothing was helping, and I became more depressed. At first my co-workers had great compassion for my suffering. But at some point they did not want to take on more of my workload or hear about my pain. I started to feel very isolated as I watched my friends enjoying life, and I did not share in their experience.

One night, to my surprise, I saw myself in a dream in the living room of my house. A striking Native American man dressed in blue jeans and a blue shirt stood up and walked from behind the couch. His eyes were dark brown, and he had long black hair. He looked at me and said, "I've always lived here; you just didn't know it." Then he showed me an amazing blue rattle. It was made from materials that I have never seen, and it was an extraordinary color of blue that I can't describe. He pointed his finger at my body and he said, "You have a pain right here." Then he shook his rattle over the part of my body where I had been suffering. Within the dream I felt the pain leave and to this day the pain has not returned. Due to my experience I believe it is always worth asking for a healing dream. The key is that you must be persistent. If you need healing help, try setting an intention every night as you go to bed. State a decree, "Thank you for providing me with healing as I sleep. Thank you for healing me as I dream."

Once you set your intention, you might work through a deep issue in a dream. You might receive a dream that shares great wisdom about your issue. You might be shown the cause of an emotional or physical issue that provides a diagnosis that has been missed by the professionals you work with. You might wake up feeling transformed in some way although you do not have a memory of the dream.

In my dreams I am sometimes guided to take a supplement. Faye shared a similar experience with me. She had picked up a bug while traveling. She asked for a healing dream and in the dream was told that she needed to take allium. Upon awakening she looked up what allium is and learned it is garlic. She followed the advice given and added garlic to her diet.

Years ago I had gotten a terrible case of food poisoning while traveling. The medication I was taking was only helping to a point. One of my helping spirits is Snake. Snake does not show up in my journeys. But I know Snake is one of my guardian spirits who is around me at all times. Snake often shows up as an omen when I walk. And Snake shows up frequently in my dreams and always provides me with help and wisdom when she does appear.

While I was dealing with physical issues from my food poisoning, Snake showed up one night in a dream, and she bit my hand.

The surprise for me is how much this hurt in my dream. I have been bitten by Snake before in my dreams—always in the spirit of healing—never to do harm. I kept saying in my dream, "This really hurts!" When I woke up the next day I told my husband, who is an acupuncturist, about the dream. He asked me where Snake bit me. He shared with me that Snake bit me on the acupuncture meridian that went with my intestinal problem. My symptoms disappeared after this dream.

Just as you might receive a spontaneous healing in a journey, the same might occur in a dream. Fred received a soul retrieval in a dream where he received back parts of himself that he lost during his time in the military. Linda experienced a shamanic extraction in a dream where an intrusive energy was removed that was causing her severe neck pain. As with journeying these dreams occur when we are ready to receive a deep and life-changing healing.

DREAMS TEACH THROUGH METAPHOR

Dreams are typically metaphorical. People often have dreams about their house or car that symbolizes a physical issue. A garden in need of care might be shown as a way to describe an issue that needs to be addressed.

Dave had a dream about his house. In the dream he was shown how he needed to fix certain rooms that had moved into a state of deterioration and disrepair. When he woke up, the meaning of the dream was very clear to him. He knew he was living a life filled with a great deal of stress. He was not attentive to his body, did not eat well, and rarely exercised. Dave knew that the dream was showing him that he had to pay more attention to fixing his body, so that like a house, it did not go too far into a state of deterioration.

Sometimes it is very obvious what the metaphor you receive in a dream is pointing to. And sometimes you might wake up with no comprehension of the meaning of a dream. You will find that a journey to your helping spirits can assist you in interpreting a dream.

HEALING ON ALL LEVELS

I encourage you to remain open to how the spirits can heal during journeying and sleeping, and in the course of your daily life. Sometimes you might not even remember the healing source, for the healing can go so deep into the psyche that the unconscious takes in the healing, without the conscious mind needing to hold onto the details or even be aware of what occurred.

Of course as with any traditional or alternative practice *a cure* cannot be promised. For many of us the process of going through the challenge, learning what changes we need to make in our life and what wounds, life situations, and events need healing ends up providing a tremendous amount of growth and evolution. If a challenge is taken away without the deep inner personal work being accomplished, another similar challenge might appear later on. When you combine asking for healing help while also doing your personal inner work, you can create long-term healing in your life.

You are gaining tools to live a harmonious and spiritual life. Emotional and physical challenges appear as you are led to explore the depth of your inner landscape and make the necessary changes to create a healthy inner garden.

7

Initiations of Death and Rebirth

AT THIS POINT YOU MIGHT take some time to reflect on times in your life when so much change occurred that you literally felt aspects of your former self drop away. During this time you might have felt you were being reshaped into a new being, filled with greater wisdom, strength, humility, and compassion. As we grow into "wiser" beings, we come to realize that our grief about what was lost actually led us to becoming healthier people. While you go through the process, you cannot see the end. Learning how to ride out these initiations we go through during such an intense time of transformation on the planet is key to living a conscious life.

The challenges that life brings to us lead to a rite of passage, which is an initiation. Initiation marks a change. We all go through initiatory experiences on a regular basis; life is filled with change. Some examples might be a separation or divorce, death of a loved one, recovering from an illness, losing a job, children leaving home, or moving into a new house. There are the initiations that occur when an aspect of our personality or way of being in the world no longer serves us. Every change that we experience in life marks a death, a death of an old way of life.

In shamanic cultures, death is not feared. Death is not seen as an end—death is a rite of passage, an initiation. Death is a transition that gives birth to something new. It marks a new time in life. A rebirth occurs following each transition.

There is the big death that we experience at the end of our lives and the little deaths that life brings as we experience change. Death leads to a state of expansion where we transcend a limited perception, a limited consciousness. Death opens us to a whole new way of being in the world, shifting us into a new consciousness and with expanded perception. Throughout our lives, life itself and the power of the universe sculpt us, helping us to evolve into beings that are greater than what we were before. We let go of old beliefs, old ways of living, and old personality traits so that we open up to a new expanded consciousness and a new level of awareness. The purpose of initiation is to carve away what is on the surface of our ego and personality so that the depth of spirit can shine through. Life provides initiations on its own. While we don't need to ask for an initiation, in shamanic cultures there were formal rites of passages created to mark a life transition. The most important of these is the coming of age.

RITE OF PASSAGE INTO ADULTHOOD

In a shamanic culture a formal initiation was provided as one moved from childhood to adulthood. I have been training shamanic teachers in order to seed local communities with well-trained teachers. We have a Yahoo group where teachers I have trained have the opportunity to discuss their thoughts, their experiences, and their explorations of bridging shamanism into our culture. One issue that has raised a wealth of deep and rich discussion has to do with whether as teachers it is our responsibility to create initiatory experiences for students. There is not a black-and-white answer to this question as there are many ways to look at initiation.

There is an acceleration of violence among our youth. Suicide levels among a younger population are alarming. As we continue to watch children and teens act out with an increasing level of violence harming themselves and others, the need to create formal rite of passage ceremonies is worth exploring. There is a proverb in Africa: "If the youth are not initiated, they will burn down the village." Some facilitation into adulthood is needed.

David Tacey wrote a brilliant book titled *Gods and Diseases.* In the book he talks about a conversation he had with an Aboriginal elder Charles Ilyatjari. Charles Ilyatjari is a *ngankari,* or spirit doctor of the Pitjantjatjara people. Tacey asked him about the high rate of suicide among adolescents in his community and what his thoughts were on this. Ilyatjari responded, "There is too much worry about preventing suicide, and not enough worry about showing these boys how to die in ceremony. If we show them how to die in ceremony, their living takes care of itself."[1]

As we no longer bring formal initiation ceremonies to our youth, we might not provide them with the tools needed to navigate life. Many youth do not discover their gifts and the vision of their role in the communities they live in. As we watch the popularity in younger generations of body piercing and getting tattoos, there seems to be a desire to create a scar or sign that shows they have lived through an initiation. There is a desire to belong to community. We watch helplessly as younger members of our community engage in risky behaviors, mutilate their body, and abuse drugs. We are seeing so many youth join gangs as a way to be part of a community and to go through rites of passage together.

As a society we can lead young adults in healthy ceremonies leading to a healthier way of life. Going through an initiation experience is important for the health of the young transitioning into adulthood. As adults embarking on a spiritual path, experiencing a formal practice of initiation also helps to give tools to maneuver the transitions of life. David Tacey writes, "Our life-transitions are no longer sacred but profane or pathological. We no longer have painful initiations supervised by elders but personal traumas, crises, and meltdowns. We no longer have initiatory 'deaths,' but are plagued by suicidal thoughts, bouts of depression, burnout, and self-doubt."[2]

When an initiate went through a formal rite of passage ceremony, he or she learned the role that he played in the well-being of the community. The initiate had the opportunity to discover his or her unique gifts that added to the wholeness of the community. David Tracey plants the seed that we need to make the transition from innocence to responsibility. He also shares, "Something in us knows that we have to die, be displaced, or interrupted, so that a greater life can emerge."[3]

THE SHAMAN'S DEATH

The initiation for many shamans came through life itself. A near death experience, a life threatening illness, or a psychotic break might occur where the initiate heals from the experience returning with the knowledge of being one with Source and the power of the universe. This was called *the shaman's death.*

Many of us can relate to the shaman's death. We might suffer an illness that leads us to let go of our old life and way of being in the world. Or many of us lose so much of our old life through loss of a close relationship, losing a job, or home that we feel like a snake shedding its skin. There are no safety nets during the shaman's death. Our life is dismembered. During these times we feel like we might not live through all that life is bringing to us. Over time we learn that these intense initiations actually create a healthier life.

In such an initiation you lose your identity that you are so attached to as a personality. The re-memberment that takes place over time is where your old identity is replaced with your authentic self. Life circumstances that provide such death experiences can oftentimes seem very harsh, but in the end, once you surrender to what your new identity is, you emerge reborn and refreshed.

During a time of great emotional turmoil in my life, I asked my teacher Isis in a journey what was happening. She turned to me and said, "You are going through an initiation." I responded, "I don't think I am going to live through it." Isis looked at me with loving eyes filled with compassion, yet with a very stern voice said, "If you thought you were going to live through it, it would not be an initiation."

Whether an initiation comes through surviving a trauma or through having a blissful connection with the divine, it is a powerful time of rebirth as you step into a new way of perceiving yourself and the world. You might feel fragile for a while. It is important to nurture yourself in healthy ways. Tell friends and family that you need some loving gentle care. Ask your loved ones to have patience. Your helping spirits can provide guidance on how to nurture and take care of yourself.

DISMEMBERMENT IN SHAMANISM AND WORLD RELIGIONS

Most world religions refer to dismemberment as a way of speaking about the death of the ego that must die to experience the connection with spirit. In Buddhist meditation, dismemberment is used to dissolve limitations of the mind. In the Hindu tradition, Kali is seen as the creator and destroyer—before we can create the new, we must destroy the old. By letting go of our material nature, we can be one with the divine and eternal life. The Kabbalists teach about "the rung of nothingness," the state before creation where the egg has disappeared but the chick has not formed. In alchemy it is taught that the self-possessed man must die for the Great Work to be done. The Great Work refers to living a life in unity with the divine. Carl Jung wrote about dismemberment dreams. He shared that it is common for children to have dismemberment dreams, creating a shift of perception and a shift of awareness. This marked a rite of passage leading the child into a spiritual way of life.

In shamanic cultures a vision or journey of dismemberment was not asked for. The experience came spontaneously. If a person reported to the community that he had a dismemberment dream or some vision of dismemberment, he was viewed as a shaman. For in the practice of shamanism, it is believed that the shaman's healing gifts come after he goes through a dismemberment, experiencing unity consciousness where he becomes a hollow bone and vessel for healing energies.

Dismemberment marks a time when one now steps onto a spiritual path. Dismemberment can be life changing as we experience ourselves as one with the web of life, and we lose any sense of separation. Yes, we come back again as a personality, but we hold in our cells, in our cellular memory, the truth of who we are. The truth of who we are is divine light and love. We are connected fully to the web of life. There is no separation, there's only connection.

Dismemberment is a journey of transformation that leads us to be able to express ourselves more fully in the world. It is an experience of purification and liberation that helps us transcend the usual way of perceiving reality.

Belgium physicist, Ilya Prigogine won a Nobel Prize in 1977 for his theory of dissipative structures, a kind of chaos theory. He showed that a period of dissolution is necessary before any system—a cell, a person, society, or solar system—can jump to a higher level of organization. Seen this way, unraveling, disintegration, or dismemberment is a vital creative event making room for the new.

Dismemberment is a spiritual rebirth. The rebirth can occur through a shift in consciousness, but it can also occur through the miraculous healing that takes place during a dismemberment journey, dream, or vision. And in the experience of dismemberment, you can feel your luminosity that goes beyond a thinking state to where you fully embrace and embody the radiant being you truly are. It can truly be a numinous experience.

In his book *The Unfolding Self,* Ralph Metzner shares some of Knud Rasmussen's experiences, a well-known explorer. Rasmussen heard an Eskimo shaman saying, "Every real shaman has to feel *qaumaneg,* a light within the body, inside his head or brain, something like fire, that enables him to see in the dark, and with closed eyes see into things that are hidden, and also into the future."[4] This experience of light comes after some form of dismemberment occurs.

Anthropologist Larry Peters shares that after a dismemberment, Eskimo shamans are filled with light, giving them their psychic and healing abilities. For Aboriginal shamans in Australia a luminous quartz crystal might be placed in their body by the celestial great god, allowing them flight to heaven. Experiences of being transformed by light are spoken of among shamans in Siberia, Malaysia, and North and South America. Mircea Eliade says this experience of light changes human existence by creating a spiritual rebirth, opening one to the world of spirit.[5] In a dismemberment, the initiate lets go of everything that keeps him from experiencing unity with the universe and the web of life. In the dream or vision, the shaman experiences himself as a being of spiritual light and radiating unconditional love.

DISMEMBERMENT IN YOUR LIFE

There are initiatory experiences one can go through that involve fasting, being scarred in some way, and vision questing. For the purpose of introducing you to this topic, I am presenting a practice that you can choose to engage in that has used been used in many shamanic cultures. I will guide you to experience a dismemberment within a shamanic journey. In such a journey you let go of your body, your mind, and your personality. You drop the aspect of yourself that experiences separation from the universe and the rest of life. This type of journey leads you into unity consciousness where you experience who you are beyond your skin.

An experience of dismemberment can occur in a journey by your request. The process of dismemberment in a journey can also happen spontaneously. In this type of journey a helping spirit might dismember you or call in a force of nature or another animal to perform the work to help you shed whatever keeps you separate from the power of the universe. Dismemberment sculpts away the ego so that you can truly experience your true spiritual nature and identity.

In a dismemberment journey you are devoured spiritually and cleansed by helping spirits so that what no longer serves you in your life is removed. You are unburdened by blocks that prevent you from moving forward in the next phase of your soul's journey. The process entails disintegration, illumination, remembering, reconstruction, and re-emergence. When you feel ready you can perform a journey and set your intention to ask a helping spirit to assist you in being dismembered. This could end up being a healing for you.

Your skin might be eaten, and you are reduced to bone.

You might even be burned to ash. Organs might be washed
or replaced with crystals.

As your skin and organs are removed, an emotional or
physical illness could also be removed.

At the end of the journey you are reassembled. Healing takes place as
your organs and bones are cleansed and your body is reconstructed
without your former illness. Your body is reconstructed with health
and vitality and with a consciousness that embraces unity with all of
life. This leads to a feeling of healing and revitalization. In shamanic
cultures it was seen that the initiate acquired his or her psychic gifts
and healing powers through such an experience.

Bob was a student of mine who had suffered multiple traumas in
his life. He suffered from PTSD after serving in the military during
the Vietnam War. During his very first shamanic journey, he was met
by a lion, who introduced himself as Bob's power animal. The lion
proceeded to rip Bob apart until he was a skeleton. The lion then
licked all of Bob's bones cleaned. As he reconstructed Bob by putting back his organs and body parts, he filled all of Bob's cells with
luminous light. On returning Bob felt amazed by this experience. He
had never journeyed before or heard of dismemberment. Bob felt like
a new person and continued to journey for further healing of his past
wounds. The depth of the guidance he continues to receive is a reflection of his commitment to his healing.

I have led clients on dismemberment journeys to dismember grief
after losing a loved one. You can also journey to ask a helping spirit
to dismember a fear, disappointment, or anger. You can also ask your
helping spirit to dismember a physical illness you are dealing with.

In my own practice, I've asked my helping spirits for a series of
dismemberments where over time I continue to release a block or challenge. In one of my very first journeys, I visited my power animal after
I had experienced heartbreak. My power animal lovingly pushed me
into a campfire. I was burned down to ash and then re-membered
without the intensity of my grief. With a dismemberment journey

where you ask for grief, fear, anger, disappointment, or other challenging emotional states to be dismembered, the results might not lead to an immediate clearing of these emotions. But this journey begins a healing process that continues over time, for once we state an intention that we are asking to be healed, the universe starts to answer our call in a variety ways.

I request a dismemberment journey during times when I am experiencing illness or fatigue. At the end of the journey I ask to be re-membered with the spiritual strength of my teacher Isis. In this way I am renewed and refreshed with the power of the universe. I encourage you to try this in your practice where at the end of your journey you ask to be filled with the spiritual power of one of your helping spirits.

At times, the initiate might not be reconstructed or re-membered at the end of the visionary experience. It was understood that when remaining in a dismembered state, the helping spirits would continue to work on the initiate's state of being so that he or she would metaphorically "percolate," "cook," or "simmer" while greater work on his consciousness was being done. The re-memberment might occur days, weeks, months, or longer after the initial experience.

JOURNEY TO ASK FOR A DISMEMBERMENT

You might need a longer time for this journey. Take your time and find a musical track that you can journey to for fifteen to thirty minutes. The intention for this journey is to visit your power animal, guardian spirit, or teacher in the Lower or Upper World and ask to be dismembered and re-membered. You can focus on an emotional blockage or physical challenge that you wish to release.

In this journey, it is most important to be willing to surrender to the universe and trust the powers that be to provide you with what is needed for your healing, growth, and evolution. Let your helping spirit set the stage. It might perform the dismemberment. It might call in another animal or an element, such as a bear, an eagle, a sandstorm, or fire to provide the dismemberment.

Surrender to your helping spirit as it creates an experience to help you release that which keeps you separate from the universe. Trust your helping spirit.

Some dismemberment stories sound quite gruesome, but with all of the people I've trained, the experience of dismemberment is reported as a pleasant and loving experience. There is a sense of relief as you let go of your burdens. There is a sense of calm and peace as you once again experience your connection to all of life, the power and creative force of the universe.

Surrender to the power of the universe to bring you into unity consciousness. Experience the light of who you are. You are divine light, and who you are beyond your skin is luminous. Spiritually you are connected to the web of life. And after you have experienced this state of being and have been spiritually cleansed, your helping spirit will rebuild you, leaving out any emotional or physical pain as you are reborn.

Once your journey is complete, return. Return to your starting place and then to the room you are in. Feel your connection with the earth, and also feel the earth reaching out toward you, holding you, and embracing you. Notice if you experience a sense of mental clarity. With your eyes closed, take a few deep breaths. You might feel a tingling in your body, or you might feel a pulsation of light. When you do open up your eyes, notice if the colors are clearer. Notice if your hearing is sharper or improved. Notice if any of your senses are more heightened. This can be an effect of such a healing and transformative journey. Take your time before standing up. Give yourself some space and time to allow all that has happened for you to fully sink in.

You cannot order the universe to give you a life changing and profound experience during one short journey. For some, the results can be very profound if the time is right. Some of you might need to repeat this journey. Some of you might be surprised that you receive a spontaneous dismemberment during a journey on another intention. When you hold an intention for a journey of initiation, there will be an impact on your consciousness. The process of transformation has begun.

Dismemberment journeys serve multiple purposes. They are used as an initiation allowing you to experience who you are beyond your ego and personality. Dismemberment journeys can also be used for healing.

INTEGRATING YOUR CHANGES

After you have gone through a life-changing initiation, it can be challenging to fit back into your former life. You might relate differently to your friends and loved ones. You might feel isolated as what used to be familiar now seems changed. It might feel like you are attempting to wear old clothes that no longer fit. The experience can feel like being a newborn whose skin has not thickened and is vulnerable to the energy of others. During these times you might feel fragile and need some time to grow into your new skin. You might need the help of a shamanic practitioner or the help of a therapist in making the necessary life changes that reflect back your state of growth and evolution.

You might discover a new sense of direction for your life and feel a need to integrate a new set of values. Consider changing your altar when you go through a change or initiation. In this way your altar and your sacred space reflects back your new way of living and your shift in your evolution of consciousness.

WELCOMING RETURNING INITIATES

It is interesting to note that when an individual in a community suffered from a mental or physical illness, the entire community was impacted. And this is why in many shamanic cultures the entire community showed up to support the shaman's healing work for a client. The success of the healing affected the vitality of the entire community.

In a shamanic culture the initiate was welcomed home by the elder, as well as others in the community. Stories were listened to. Deep feelings were shared and understood. There was a formal acceptance back home. I have heard stories about how the Native American communities welcomed home returning veterans from the Iraq and Afghanistan wars. There was a sweat lodge ceremony created for them where the returning veteran shared the stories of any trauma experienced. The elders and family deeply listened to the stories. And the returning veteran truly felt listened to and welcomed back home. They have a place in their community versus being treated like an outcast. Edward Tick, PhD, wrote a powerful book on the topic of helping returning veterans titled *Warrior's Return: Restoring the Soul after War.*[6]

During the discussions among my teachers on our Yahoo group, we have shared about how many returning "initiates" are often treated as "outcasts." We need to learn how to create a safe structure for returning initiates.

This holds true for those who suffered a mental illness or loss and for those who embrace an expanded awareness that was gained through a shaman's death. There is so much we can do for those suffering from mental illness, a spiritual awakening, or PTSD that we are not doing. Further discussion and knowledge is needed to create safe structures in our communities that hold the initiate in love, honor, and respect and welcome them back home again. The times we live in are calling us to heighten and expand our knowledge on just how we can create strong communities for those who need to remember their sacred place that contributes to the community at large.

The various challenges we go through in life lead us to a state of expansion and growth. In challenging times we find ourselves opening our hearts, and this expands our ability to remain in a state of compassion. We deepen who we are. Challenges are initiations that facilitate our growth toward the light.

4

CULTIVATING YOUR INNER GARDEN

CLOSE YOUR EYES AND TAKE A FEW DEEP BREATHS. Using your imagination, leave your ordinary world behind, and imagine traveling within to your Inner World to visit your inner garden. Set your intention to experience yourself as a garden.

Inspect and examine your soil. Is your soil rich? Is it fertile? Does it need water? Does it need nutrients? What is the texture of your soil? Don't judge; just observe.

Being a caretaker of your inner garden is a joyful experience. As you feel the texture of the soil, sense the excitement of the unlimited possibilities and potential of what can be grown in this vital inner garden. Healthy and strong plants grow in fertile soil. Seeds will be planted containing the program of your soul's purpose as well as how to live a life filled with passion and meaning. The seeds of your dreams will be planted of what you would like to manifest in your life and for the world. You will remove the plants that no longer serve you. The healthier your soil, the healthier your garden. The healthier your garden, the healthier your life. This is a time to feel awe, wonder, and excitement for all that you can grow and create in your life. You are the caretaker of your garden. It is up to you to feed your garden with love, nurturing the seeds so that they can grow into strong and vital plants.

Continue to breathe deeply. After examining your garden, connect with your heart. Feel the love, excitement, enthusiasm, and the energy of awe and wonder as you nurture your garden. Feel your heartbeat. Experience the energy filled with love and excitement growing. Connect your heartbeat with the heartbeat of the Earth. Merge with the heartbeat and the rhythm of the Earth. Bring yourself into alignment with the Earth. This creates a state of health and harmony. Call your helping spirits to you as you continue your work to grow, evolve, and transform your life. Take a deep breath and be here now.

8

The Destiny of Your Soul
Arises from Your Earthly Dream

IT IS ESSENTIAL TO JOURNEY to your Inner World to develop a rich inner landscape. This creates inner and outer transformation and a sense of empowerment. This leads you to a realm of understanding of *I am enough.* And when you evolve into this place, you are not so impacted by all that happens in the outer world. You begin to move through life with grace as you step into a new dimension of life.

Using the metaphor of your life as a garden is a valuable way to enliven and deepen your Inner World. We live on the Earth, which is a garden, and inside each of us is a garden that needs to be cared for and cultivated. We are caretakers of our Earth garden within and without. As you continue with the upcoming chapters, I will ask you to continue examining your inner garden. With intention you will plant seeds you wish to see grow into strong and healthy plants in your life. You will remove those plants whose roots might have grown strong and deep but no longer contribute to your health and well-being.

As I have shared, your helping spirits can guide you and can provide healing help for you, but they will not do your personal work. The realm of inner transformation and empowerment is for you to do.

YOUR STORY OF CREATION

When shamans talked about being in unity with the power of universe, Source, the gods, and goddesses, they had the sensory awareness in their body of what they were in union with. In our culture, this teaching of becoming one with Source often remains a mental concept. And if it's only a mental concept, then you won't get the true experience of what it means to move through life carried by your spirit.

In indigenous cultures people had creation stories, creation myths. It was through these creation stories that people truly understood on a cellular and kinesthetic level the creative force they were connected to. They experienced the unconditional love of their creator. This helped shamans, healers, and mystics to be a vessel of love and light in their communities.

We practice different religious traditions. We have different religious beliefs. Therefore, it is impossible for us to have one creation story. But in reality, indigenous cultures did not embrace just one creation story. As it was recognized that there was a rich variety of creation stories, people would gather to listen to a wealth of different myths. Instead of comparing stories, people would remark on how beautiful each story was. In life there are many philosophical questions we hold. Some people turn to religion and society to provide answers to the mysteries of the universe. Some people search throughout their lives to find answers for themselves through a practice of direct revelation.

One question is: Where do we come from? There is a need to address the issue beyond the biological response. Native cultures have creation stories, which give a foundation of how life on Earth was created. These stories help to create a map for how to live life. These stories help to connect the soul to spirit, as we all search for a deeper connection that enriches and enlivens our inner landscape.

Although you might have been taught a creation story in your religious upbringing, you must ask yourself if this story provides you insight on how to be creative in life and connects your soul to your spirit. It is important to have a direct experience of meeting your creator and learning how you and the world were created. You have to find the words for the creator that fit into your belief—God, the goddess, the power of the universe, Source, and so on.

JOURNEY TO EXPERIENCE A CREATION STORY

Start by preparing for your journeywork. Use the form of music and journeying that works best for you. Find a comfortable place to journey, and you can place a cover over your eyes. Many prefer to dance while performing this journey. In this journey your intention is to explore the power of creation.

You might find that you need to journey separately on these steps. Hold the intention that you wish to meet your creator to learn about your own personal story of creation, to learn who your creator is, to find out the details of your story of creation. Learn for yourself, explore for yourself how the world was created. This is what myths are created from.

There are two other very important parts of this journey. Ask to experience how much love went into your creation. This is a life-altering experience for many who did not experience true unconditional love from their parents. Please know you were created from a place of unconditional love. In the journey you want to absorb into your cells fully the love that went into your creation. As you absorb the love and light of your creator, your own internal light will continue to grow and shine through you. In computer terminology, receive a download of love.

Next go beyond the story of your creation and ask to experience the energy that went into creation. Feel the pure raw energy of creation without any form or trying to understand the hows and whys of creation. There is an energy behind creation that is beyond words and that cannot be rationally understood. Dropping the words and experiencing the energy behind the story allows you to get a transmission that speaks to the depth of your soul. This is such an incredible force to experience and will inform you in very deep ways of how much energy is required to create the life you desire.

When you feel ready, return by leaving the spiritual landscape you are in. You can always return at another time to access more information. Retrace your steps and return to your room. Feel your body and open your eyes. Look around you and take in the visual details of the room you are in. Feel your body against the material you are sitting or lying on. Or feel the floor beneath you if you were dancing. Wiggle your fingers and toes. Take a deep breath and notice the air traveling into and through your lungs. Be fully present now.

INTEGRATING AND EXPRESSING YOUR CREATION STORY

When you feel and express this limitless and bountiful energy, you will experience the magic of the energy behind the methods, techniques, and practices you work with. You will now have a sense of the love and the energetic momentum that goes into healing and also creating the life you wish to live. Take some to write out your story of creation. Don't simply record what happened in the journey. Rather, write a creation myth. Next draw a symbol of your creator that allows you to experience the creator's unlimited power. Sometimes we get very attached to the form and the identity of our creator as we often do with our helping spirits. For example, you might see a power animal as a wolf or a teacher who appears as Quan Yin. In reality our power animals and teachers are formless and unlimited energy. The same is true for the creative force of the universe. This force is so expansive it cannot be limited by any kind of form.

Draw a symbol of your creator that might be a beautiful reflection of how unlimited the power is. For example, you might draw a symbol of light that has rays that shine into infinity.

Express the energy that went into creation in a drawing. You might do a separate drawing to let this energy and power flow into colors and shapes. You can express this energy by dancing, singing, or engaging in a craft to make something in the material world that holds unlimited power.

Another way to do this work is to use the practice of automatic writing. To engage in this process find a piece of music that expands and heightens your consciousness. Write your intention down on a piece of paper. Next close your eyes half way and as you listen to the music allow your pen or pencil to move across the paper. At first you might feel your writing is a bit forced. But as you continue, you will find your inner spirit taking over, and your pen or pencil will glide across the page. Words and a story will come through you, emerging from a deep place of knowing instead of simply repeating rational information that is already in your conscious mind. Don't worry whether or not you are writing in a straight line. Just allow your words to flow through you.

At some point you will want to take the time to simply close your eyes and experience the love that went into your creation and the pure energy that went into creation.

I have journeyed to meet my creator multiple times. Every time I perform this journey, I experience a different aspect of my creation story. My helping spirit asks me to reflect on how a diamond has different facets to it. The creative force of the universe is multifaceted too. And with each symbol that I draw, I hang these pictures on the walls of my office so that I have a reflection I can gaze upon when I forget the truth of who I am. During a difficult phone conversation, all I have to do is look up and be reminded that my creator is pure light and I am pure light, too. This reminder helps me shift my perception and shift into a higher level of consciousness, which allows my words and behavior to be a reflection of love.

YOUR CREATION AS AN ACT OF LOVE

I suggest that you repeat this journey to deepen your experience of the love and energy that went into creation. As you continue to feel the love that went into your creation, you will acknowledge that you deserve the best that life has to offer. So many of us feel that we don't deserve to be happy, or we feel insecure about our gifts and abilities. But to truly know how much love you were created with transforms these self-sabotaging attitudes. When you love yourself unconditionally, you start to trust yourself. You stop trying to please others and no longer have a need for outside recognition. What becomes important is following what your soul is truly calling you to do that will lead to your ultimate happiness.

Lily struggled with deep depression. She had been abused by her alcoholic father. And she never felt loved by her mother. It was hard for Lily to find any joy or meaning in her life. She was committed to healing her past, and she had made a tremendous amount of progress when I met her. But what catapulted her into the next step of healing was experiencing how much love went into her creation. Just being able to experience this fully throughout her body changed everything for her. Although she acknowledged the suffering she went through as a child, she had a new and strong foundation to work from that helped her to create a new story to create a positive future for herself.

Over time you will deepen your understanding that you are a reflection of your creator and the creative forces of the universe. This knowledge will help to fuel your own creative abilities and potential.

FINDING MEANING IN YOUR LIFE

Life without meaning leads to a life of despair. Many people keep to the status quo, which does not lead to a meaningful life, leaving them feeling empty. It is important to discover what you are passionate about doing, what activities have meaning for you. Loving your life helps to pull you out of the darkness. Isis has shared with me that the love for life will always light the way, carrying you through turbulent times. When we dull ourselves and lose passion for life, the light starts to go out of our eyes. When the light goes out of our eyes, the light also goes out of the Earth.

In the early 1990s I was performing a soul retrieval ceremony for a client to have return to him parts of his soul lost at a traumatic time of his life. During the journey my power animal led me in a most unexpected fashion. He took me back to view the spirit of this man before he was born. He showed me, as a spirit, the decision he made of the gift, the talent, and strength he wanted to manifest in this lifetime. I was shown what he really wanted to do with his life and the destiny of his soul. I was shown who he was before other people started projecting their own expectations onto him.

At this point I asked my power animal, "How did he lose this excitement and knowledge?" As I was performing a soul retrieval, I needed further instructions on how to proceed with this other aspect of the work. My power animal responded to me and said, "He never lost this knowledge, rather he *forgot* why he came here." I responded with, "Well, if he didn't lose it, how am I supposed to bring it back?" He showed me a symbol that represented the gift and the strength of this man. He instructed me to blow this symbol into the heart of my client, and he called this process *soul remembering*. Over the years, soul remembering became a predominant ceremony in my work with clients. I have written and taught extensively on the topic.

I started to reflect very deeply on how, as human beings, we project expectations and what we perceive onto other people. We see other people through our own eyes, but we don't always see who a person really is. I remembered when I was just a young child, I realized that nobody was actually going to see me for who I really was. This was a profound realization to have at such a young age. We are born with a gift, talent, strength, or passion we want to express. Then our parents and other authority figures start to project onto us what they think we are gifted at. We take intelligence tests, and we are told what we are good at doing. I have worked with many people whose parents told them, "You will be a great doctor or lawyer when you grow up." They never really had a chance to go inside and ask, "What is *my* excitement, what do *I* really want to do and express in this lifetime?"

We often end up forgetting why we came here. We take on roles that we don't even feel connected to. Our creative fire is dampened. When we do not have *passion* for what we are doing in life, when we don't have that *excitement* for what life is about, we start to move into a place of depression and despair, which is an issue for so many. When we find what we are passionate about doing, we regain a sense of hope that fuels our creative potential.

I received a very powerful message while working with a client who had suffered multiple life-threatening illnesses in her lifetime. When I performed her soul retrieval, my power animal shared an important teaching. He explained that her illness was caused by apathy and her cure was passion. He went on to share that my client's lesson in this lifetime was to learn what happens if another life-form in her body had more passion for life than she did: the virus or bacteria would thrive.

This is a potent teaching. Viruses and bacteria seem to have great intelligence about how to mutate to deal with the modern-day medications being used against them. Based on the increasing mutations of disease we are seeing, it seems like viruses and bacteria are more passionate about life than we are, for when you look into the eyes of people, many do not have passion for life shining through their eyes. We need to match the learning curve of viruses and bacteria and find our passion, excitement, love for life, hope, and radiance to thrive.

This next journey is to help you remember your soul's purpose. An alternative to performing a shamanic journey is taking a walk in nature while focusing on the intention to learn about your soul's destiny. Notice what emerges from the deep well inside you as you walk in silence surrounded by the beauty of nature.

JOURNEY TO DISCOVER WHAT
YOU ARE HERE TO MANIFEST

Find a comfortable place to journey where you won't be disturbed. If you choose to, put something over your eyes, and set your intention to travel back in time to when you were considering taking on a body. Your intention is to discover your destiny and what you came here to manifest in your lifetime.

Imagine being a spark of light considering taking a body on this great planet. You look down at the Earth, perceiving the incredible beauty of this planet. Remember, spirits don't get to see brilliant colors or eat sweets and tasty food. Spirits don't get to smell the fragrances of roses. Spirits don't get to touch or experience the wealth of feelings we do. The entire range of experiences of being a sensory being, being able to see the beauty of colors, smell fragrances, feel emotions, touch, hear the sounds of nature, and taste incredible food is something you get to experience as being human.

Before you were born into this world, there was something you were excited about experiencing and expressing during your lifetime. Once you were born, other people started to project onto you. What was your original excitement about being born? What was that gift, talent, strength, passion you came into this world to express? Learn what your destiny is, what you came here to do. Ask to be shown your soul's purpose.

When you have received a glimpse into your soul's purpose, return from the journey. Feel power and the life force, excitement, creative energy, and passion moving through you. This marks an initiation as you rediscover how your creative fire can be reignited by living a life filled with passion and meaning.

Once back you can write out your experience of this journey. Find some drawing materials, and draw a symbol that is a metaphor that represents the gift, talent, or strength that you came here to manifest in this lifetime. Some examples might be a star, a spiral, a peaceful lake, a strong and grounded tree, or a flame. Use your imagination. Oftentimes people don't want to do any artwork because they judge their artistic ability. We are all artists! It is about the energy that you put into the drawing that will create transformation for you. This drawing will be your true spiritual self-portrait. Carl Jung taught, "Symbols speak to our unconscious." The more that you can continue to look at this symbol and reflect on your symbol, it will start to inform your psyche so that you begin to change how you live your life. I suggest putting the drawing of this symbol up somewhere in your house or at work where you can see it again and again. You can also use the practice of automatic writing as I described previously.

SETTING REALISTIC GOALS
FOR FULFILLING YOUR PURPOSE

One key in doing this work is to start with a realistic goal. Some people get over-enthusiastic and create unrealistic goals where there are not clear steps to get from point A to B. Refine your work with this journey by asking for clear next steps that will lead you to the outcome you are seeking. Otherwise you might get paralyzed with only getting a "grand" vision without the practical steps to lead you to the meaningful life your soul is calling for.

When John performed this journey, he woke up to the fact that he was not living the life that his soul called for. He was following what his parents wanted for him and what his teachers told him he was gifted at. It took some time for him to revision what he wanted to do in life. He took sculpting a new life career for himself step by step. He continued to do the work of making slow and practical changes until he found himself stepping into a new career where he would be successful and that would feed his soul.

You might wish to keep a journal of your adventures as you embark on living a life that is filled with heart and meaning. As you write, you might find yourself inspired to try out new ideas of how you can continue to sculpt your life in new ways as you follow the depth of your soul's calling.

Part of the healing needed for the planet is for us to discover and feel our radiance. To heal yourself and the planet, it is time for you to be passionate about life and let light shine through your eyes. In this way light returns to the Earth.

9

Dreaming *into* Being
the Life You Desire

WE WOULD ALL LOVE to tap into the power to create the life that we desire. There are so many people suffering from depression, hopelessness, and despair. These states lead people to numb themselves and operate on automatic instead of tapping into the incredible creative potential that creates the force and excitement lighting up the joy of our soul. Once you have discovered what your soul is calling for, it is time to take steps that will lead you toward manifesting a life filled with meaning and passion.

THE GIFT OF OUR IMAGINATION

Imagination is the force behind how we dream and create. Imagination is a gift bestowed by our creator. Yet in a modern culture we are taught to stop using our imagination and to stop dreaming. Many of us are told at a young age, "There are only a few creative geniuses on the planet, and you are not one of them." We are encouraged to follow the rules, to do what we are supposed to do when told, not to shine our light too brightly, not to stand out, and not to dream too big. If you stand out, you will bring unwanted attention to yourself. These were some potent seeds planted in our inner garden by society and authority figures. For if we truly tapped into our creative potential, how could we be controlled?

It is time for you to engage fully in dreaming the world you wish to live in into being. This is your responsibility, and it means that you have to stimulate your ability to imagine your desired outcome. We are using our imaginations all the time to create our life. As we have not been focusing our imagination, as was taught in traditional cultures, we are dreaming into being a life of chaos and much unnecessary suffering. We have to train our imaginations to dream the best that life has to offer instead of the nightmare that so many continue to day-dream into being. In shamanic cultures it is understood that life is just a dream. Some shamans share that we are dreaming the wrong dream.

We talk about wanting to see positive change for ourselves and the planet. But we often forget that we each have a role in creating positive change. Many of us fall into a passive role and just expect some outside force to do our work. You must remember that to experience the fruit from a tree, first there is a seed planted. Out of the seed grows roots, a trunk, and branches. Then with care and nurturance, flowers grow on the branches, which yield fruit. Fruit does not just miraculously appear without the natural process of growth.

We are all responsible for dreaming positive change into manifest form. This is part of a moving from a hierarchical structure to bringing in the power of the feminine, which involves working with the power of collaboration and cooperation. Florence Scovel Shinn was a minister for the New Thought Church. She shared a wonderful teaching, "Creation comes through you not to you."

THE DREAM OF YOUR SOUL

Engaging your imagination to do your dreaming work is a very tricky topic if you are only doing the work from a place of personality and ego where you are led by "I want" and "I need" without further investigation into seeing if your desire is for your highest good and speaks to your soul. On a personality level you might want to manifest a new car or another material possession that in the end will not bring you true happiness.

At first some of my students question me and wonder if they should engage in creation work as they do not just want to create from a place of ego. On one level you have your desired outcomes, but is your desired outcome being driven only by ego? The key is to begin your dreaming work and allow it to deepen over time.

While I was writing *Walking in Light,* I had a waking dream that led me to reflect on my life and the choices I was making. I woke up in the middle of the night, and I found myself in between the worlds. I was no longer asleep, but I also was not awake. The only way I can describe my state is that I had a waking dream. In a flash I was shown the true meaning of my life. My waking dream did not last for more than one minute, if that. I was shown that the true meaning of this lifetime and what was so important to me was that I had the opportunity to see the great beauty of the Earth either through my travels, seeing photos, or watching videos of extraordinary landscapes. The message I received was that this was my first lifetime where I had the opportunity to witness the amazing landscapes of the Earth. Second, I was told that it was meaningful to me that I experienced love. And third, having the opportunity to take care of my parents at the end of their life was very important on both an emotional and soul level. I was surprised that in this flash of deep awareness nothing about my work came up. I love my work, and I do believe that it has been a true gift to be able to see clients, teach, and write. But it was also clear to me that there were other areas of my life that were important to me on a soul level.

By devoting time to your spiritual practices, you will discover new layers of yourself that take you beyond your personality to the depths of your soul. Over time you will increase your capacity to identify what has meaning to you on a deep level. Also through the guidance of your helping spirits as well as gaining life experience, you start to sort out the question of what intention to focus on while you engage in dreaming the life you wish for yourself and for the planet.

There is also a paradox that you have to dance, and it can be a challenging dance. The dance is to engage in creation and dreaming practices while letting go of the attachment to the outcome at the same time. You will need to be persistent and hold the vision of what you want to see for yourself and what you want to see for the planet while also surrendering the outcome to spirit.

DAYDREAMS

In spiritual traditions it is taught that everything that exists in the physical world begins first in the spiritual world. It is our thoughts, words, and daydreams that start in the invisible realms that manifest as form. Our thoughts, words, and daydreams are the seeds from which our earth garden grows. This next practice will be a diagnostic journey where you can learn firsthand what you have been dreaming into being with your imagination. This journey will be very enlightening for you and will assist you as you continue the work ahead.

At night we dream, but we forget that with our imagination we also dream throughout the day. You can journey to meet with the helping spirits who I call the Master or Mistress of Dreams to help you interpret a nighttime dream. In this journey you will work with the Master or Mistress of Dreams to examine your daydreams. By visiting the territory the Land of Dreams, you can meet with the Master or Mistress of Dreams to observe what you've been creating in your life with your thoughts and words. Your thoughts and words make up the daydreams that you have throughout the day. It is important to examine what seeds you are planting in your inner garden and what ends up sprouting into your life. You might need to remove some of these daydreams or nurture others. Your daydreams inform you about the personal work you need to do.

JOURNEY TO THE LAND OF DREAMS

The intention for this next journey is very simple. Hold your intention to journey to the Lower World to the Land of Dreams to meet the master or mistress of this place, and ask to be shown what your daydreams are creating and manifesting into your life.

Your intention will lead you into this territory and to the helping spirit waiting to assist you.

With the assistance of the Master or Mistress of Dreams, examine what you have been dreaming into being with the day-dreams you have throughout the day. Notice how the thoughts and words you use influence what you have created in your life. Examine what you are daydreaming from your ego. Next explore what your soul is dreaming into being.

This can be an enlightening journey to request that the Master or the Mistress of the Land of Dreams show you the difference between what your ego is daydreaming into being and what your soul is dreaming into being.

With the help of the Master or Mistress of Dreams, explore connections that you can make in how some of the people, scenarios, and events in your life are manifesting through your daydreams.

Ask for guidance on how you can change your daydreams so that you can shift the story of your life.

After you return from this journey, take some time to reflect on the insights you gained and the knowledge you received about how your daily daydreams are impacting your life.

CHANGING THE DREAM

Now that you have received a glimpse of how your daydreams have been creating certain events in your life, it is time to learn how to shift your imagination to work for you rather than against you. Dreaming work changes your story.

The future is created by what you do in the present. You must dream with the fullness of your imagination. You have to engage all of your senses. The key to using your imagination is to be able to engage your strong inner senses, seeing the vivid images of the world that you wish to live in. You need to hear the sounds of a world filled with joy, smell the fragrances of a world filled with healthy elements and life forms, and taste foods cooked with love. You must enter into and live the dream fully, and walk around feeling the textures of the world you wish to live in while at the same time feeling joy and excitement in your heart. You must dream with your entire body.

As I encouraged you to enliven your senses while doing your journey work, you need to enliven your own inner senses to do your dreaming work. We oftentimes operate through life as if we're watching life as a flat screen TV. We have to allow ourselves to be fed by our senses, and we need to allow those senses to bubble up through us. If you can't get in touch with the true power of your own vivid images, your own internal songs of creation, the beauty of the fragrances you wish to smell, the taste of healthy food grown and cooked with love, and the feeling of touching the beauty of life, there's no power in your creation. Passion and enthusiasm fuel creation. As you do your creation work to engage your senses, add the power of enthusiasm to fuel your dream.

In this next journey you will begin to do some dreaming work. I would suggest you work in partnership with your helping spirits to form your intention. Your helping spirits can show you where you might be limiting your dream and falling into the belief of scarcity. And your helping spirits will help you to avoid the trap of only dreaming what your ego desires. Sometimes my helping spirits will tell me, "What you are creating is not for your highest good." Your helping spirits will suggest how to rephrase the wording of your intention.

JOURNEY TO ENVISION THE LIFE YOU LONG FOR

Start this journey by consulting with a helping spirit to formulate a vision for the life you wish to dream into being. From a heartfelt desire that you feel passionate about, discuss with a helping spirit your desired outcome, and with its help, phrase your intention so it will serve your highest good.

Once you get clear on your intention, place yourself into the world that you wish to live in. Experience all the vivid sensations.

What would you look like?

What would the people you are with look like?

What would the landscape look like?

Let your eyes drink in all the colors.

Listen to the sounds of nature and listen to children laughing.

Listen to the conversations you are having with friends and loved ones.

Breathe deeply and smell the fragrances in the air as you live the life that you wish to be living. Is the air you are breathing moist or dry?

Feel the fragrant air fill your lungs.

Notice the sensation in your feet as you stand on the earth.

Feel your fingers touching materials, and other living beings in your dream.

Put some earth into your hands and smell the fragrance and feel the texture.

Imagine eating and tasting healthy food and drinking clean fresh water.

Put some food into your mouth and fully take in all the flavors.

Take a sip of water and feel the fresh cool taste on your tongue and swallow it, noticing the sensation as the water runs downs your mouth into your throat.

A key to the practice is make sure you have stepped fully into the dream, and you are living in it with full sensory awareness. Do not observe the dream as if you are watching TV or a movie. Step into the dream, live the dream, learn from the dream as it is happening now.

Feel the excitement of your success. Experience in the journey other people saying to you, "Congratulations in manifesting your dream!" Experience the love, light, harmony, beauty, and peace that you feel inside and what is being reflected back to you in your outer world.

Dreaming work is very important to keep up throughout the day. Remember you daydream throughout the day, so train your imagination to focus on what you want. We all have times during the day when we relax and drink a cup of tea or coffee and daydream. This is a fertile time to focus on your dreaming work by using your imagination as you daydream. Engage all your inner senses to see, hear, feel, taste, and smell the world you are creating for yourself. Sculpt your daydreams as if your dream has already manifested and is here now. Otherwise you are only dreaming of an unreachable future instead of the present. The future is created from the present.

A potent time to engage in your dreaming work is right before you drift off into sleep or while you are walking in nature. You can also continue to do this practice in a journey. I find it easier to fully inhabit and occupy the space of my dream in a journey. Within a journey I can sink fully into what it's like to live from the dream.

THE VOID IS FERTILE GROUND FOR CREATION

When I journey to who I am beyond my skin, traveling deep within to my spirit, I experience the void. The void is a place of complete darkness and is the place prior to form and creation. I experience my true spiritual nature as the void. In Buddhist practices the void is described as empty yet full.

The void is fertile ground, for it is the place before thought. It is a vast territory of formlessness. The void is the place of unlimited possibilities and *unpotentiated energy*—a term I love to use to describe all the unlimited energy available that is yet to be manifested. All matter and form is birthed from the void.

JOURNEY INTO THE VOID

An alternative way to do your dreaming practices is to set your intention to journey into the void. Experience your starting place in the Middle World. Set your intention that you wish to enter the void, the place before creation. You can ask a helping spirit to escort you to the void. Or you might find that your intention takes you there. The void might be in the Upper World. I have also journeyed to the void by traveling into my Inner World. In this way of working, you use your intention to travel into the unseen realms that exist within. I find this to be a potent place in which to do my dreaming work.

Once in this territory of unpotentiated energy and unlimited possibilities, you can form your dream as described earlier. Experience your dream with all your senses. When the dream is formed, let it birth and emerge into the world, and then engage your imagination as you continue to live from the dream.

PATIENCE, PERSISTENCE, AND SURRENDER

The practice of dreaming requires patience because you need to give the proper time for your dreams to gestate. And it requires persistence because you need to repeat your dreaming work until it manifests into form. Working over time continues to fuel your intention, providing it with the needed energy to manifest your desired outcome.

Focus is essential in doing this work. In life you have to stay on the road while driving. A train must run on the tracks. In the same way it is important to keep your focus on the road ahead. There might be obstacles and turbulent times along the way, but you must keep your focus on your destination. Remember you must fully inhabit and occupy the space of the life you are dreaming into being.

You will find that you are successful in manifesting some of your dreams almost spontaneously. Some dreams, like some plants and trees, are slow to grow. Rebecca found that when she performed her dreaming work, she easily created a new job that she was passionate about doing. But where she got stuck was in manifesting a deep and meaningful partner to share her life with. Rebecca started to lose faith in herself and in the work. She would start her work and then give up. She needed to get to a place of realizing that she had further emotional work to do as she felt that on an unconscious level she was not ready for the relationship she was seeking. She also realized that the dreaming process was not as easy as it first looked to her.

Over time Rebecca made a clear choice. She decided she did not want to give up on her dream. She explored the issues that might be blocking her ability to use her creative energy. Rebecca surrendered to the universe around the right timing. In the end she found a wonderful man to share her life with. But it took making a clear choice not to give up, exploring emotional issues that needed to be healed, and being diligent and persistent with her dreaming work.

LETTING THE DREAM GO

I have found in my own life that sometimes I have a spontaneous beautiful and powerful daydream, and then I forget about it. In some ways I let the dream go, and it travels off into the universe. Suddenly and unexpectedly the dream manifests within a matter of days. I am always surprised when this happens. And typically it was not even a dream I was ready for. As this has happened numerous times in my life, I have come to understand that a potent combination is to perform my dreaming work and then to let the dream go. It ascends like a balloon flying up through the ethers to connect with universal powers that work with me in partnership to make the dream so.

What I have learned from this powerful process is to make sure I am clear on my intention. For sometimes you plant such a strong seed of intention in your inner garden, it can germinate and grow at an extremely fast pace. Working in a disciplined way with intention is so important with your dreaming work.

When your outcomes aren't manifesting in the way or in the timing that you wish them to, there will be times when you need to journey to a power animal or teacher to get guidance on dealing with the disappointment. Remember there is a paradox between holding a vision and surrendering to spirit for what is for the highest good for yourself and the planet.

As we grow and evolve and the Earth does the same, we do not know what the final outcome will be. But the world needs dreamers right now. Otherwise the chaotic dreams of our time will continue to manifest. You must continue to look at whether you are following the stream of ego or following the path of spirit. Your ego doesn't always know what is the best for you. Sometimes you cannot see the bigger picture. Learning how to cooperate with change versus resisting change and to be persistent while surrendering the outcome are part of your work. You need to learn how to allow spirit to inform you. The paradox is holding a vision while surrendering to spirit at the same time. You cannot say that you will only engage in the work if you "magically" see an immediate positive outcome. Focus on your spiritual work while understanding your desired outcome for the planet might not manifest in your lifetime.

WORKING WITH FEELINGS OF SCARCITY

The belief in scarcity is an issue that must be addressed as you continue to explore dreaming the world you wish to live in into being. A conditioned belief we hold in our culture is that there is scarcity and not enough resources for all. Many believe that there will always be people who have all they desire while others will suffer a scarcity of resources. We believe there is a scarcity of resources in nature.

Why would the creator dream into being a world filled with fear and scarcity? The question can be argued for hours through metaphysical and philosophical conversations. But as shamanism is a practice of direct revelation, I want to plant seeds of new ideas for you to reflect on and journey about. Years ago Isis encouraged me to reflect on the question, "Would a loving creator program you with fear and a belief in scarcity? Or would a loving creator program you with joy and plenty?" The program you were born with is the genetic coding or the blueprint that was instilled in you before birth. You are like a seed that is born with all the information needed to thrive.

Imagine a seed in a garden programmed with fear. What grows?

Imagine a seed programmed with scarcity. What grows?

Imagine a seed programmed with joy and abundance. What grows?

For many of us our foundation is fear and everything is built and grown out of fear. When you can experience in your cells the love that went into your creation—as you did in the last chapter—you discover how you were programmed to feel love, joy, and all the knowledge needed to create health and abundance. I have had many deep and profound journeys of observing how thought forms like this begin to take shape in the void. I watch how once a thought is formed, an undulating movement occurs releasing it from the void, birthing form into the world.

There is no scarcity in the void. There is no scarcity in the world of spirit. In spirit and in the void there are only possibilities. The concept of scarcity is man-made, and the seed that society planted in us that there *is not enough* runs deep within our core.

Does the belief in scarcity serve you? And if it does serve you, reflect on how it serves. What I have come to realize is that our belief in scarcity fuels our desire and hunger to gather more on the material level. If you think there is not enough, then you might fear not having what you need, leaving you hungry for more on a material level. When you know there is abundance of everything you need, you don't desire much. If you could manifest everything you desire for the rest of your life, you would find that your wants and needs simplify dramatically. It is the belief that there is not enough that creates the hunger and desire for more.

THE ABUNDANCE OF OUR UNIVERSE

The feminine teaches that we live in an abundant universe. And when we align with our inner divine spirit and the helping spirits, we can manifest what we need and what is for our highest good.

The people in Findhorn, Scotland, working in partnership with the Hidden Folk, grew healthy plants and vegetables out of sand and in adverse conditions. This is a true teaching of how when we align with spiritual forces, all is possible even when conditions do not seem right to our rational and conditioned mind. For in the world of spirit, there is only abundance. The creator and the helping spirits join and work with us in the spirit of collaboration and cooperation. In this way we work in partnership with spiritual forces to manifest what we need. First we must be open to spirit and live a life filled with gratitude, honor, and respect for the Earth, which is our home.

Your life experience might have shown you that there is not enough. The energy and thought forms about scarcity might have been fed through beliefs planted in you by society. And the beliefs might have grown so strong that patience and persistence are needed to create a pathway to experience the abundance that life has to offer. Reflect on what you learned about the unconditional love and pure energy that went into your creation. This will inspire you to explore your creative potential.

JOURNEYS TO LEARN ABOUT ABUNDANCE AND UNPOTENTIATED ENERGY

You can set an intention to journey into the invisible realms to meet with the Master or Mistress of Abundance. Ask this helping spirit how you can tap into the energy of abundance. Ask if there are beliefs you need to release that block you from experiencing abundance in your life.

Another very informative journey is to journey into the Middle World with the intention that you wish to merge with the seed of a favorite plant. To do this journey, use the house or space you are journeying in as your starting point. While listening to your shamanic music, experience yourself walking out the front door and into nature. State your intention that you wish to merge with a seed. You will learn about the nature of a seed by becoming it.

As you merge with the seed, learn about the blueprint it is programmed with that informs the plant how to maintain its health. All the wisdom it needs to be healthy is embedded in this blueprint. Experience the creative, potent, and unpotentiated energy contained in the seed. Experience the passion for life. You were born with the same wisdom and passion for life that is within a seed.

Using the power of intention, disengage from the seed before returning from this journey. Reflect on all that you learned.

10

Overcoming Obstacles

I LOVE TO HELP PEOPLE get in touch with their destiny, their soul's purpose, and what they came into this world to manifest. I am dedicated to helping others explore what brings passion and meaning into their lives. I am a dreamer, and my passion is to teach others the shamanic practice of dreaming to manifest the life they desire. At first there is bright spark that appears in people's eyes when they tap into the excitement that goes along with imagining the unlimited potential of what they can manifest and create.

Then I watch as the spark I witnessed is replaced with a look of concern and doubt. I watch body posture shift from sitting upright and proud to a position where the shoulders begin to droop. I observe how power begins to drain as soon as the energy of doubt emerges. At that point the word *but* begins the next sentence. The word *but* and the phrases that come next typically contain all the reasons why it is not possible to create what is desired. Each person comes up with a reason of why she cannot take the action necessary to create a life filled with passion and meaning.

Blocking beliefs begin to emerge. We have been fed so many negative attitudes throughout our lifetime. And the collective trance does not support the collective in tapping into the full creative potential available to all of us. As I shared previously, we were taught as children to follow the rules, to be part of society, to not stand out too much, and not to shine our light too brightly. Once we get really excited about our creative potential and all that we can do, suddenly the outdated sabotaging attitudes and beliefs that we absorbed gain momentum. These seeds were nurtured so well and therefore grew deep roots and into strong plants in our inner landscape. Dreaming work brings up people's insecurities about their capabilities to manifest. The work requires us to take a risk, and this can bring up the fear of failure.

It is your birthright to fully express your soul in this lifetime. You were born to do this. The creator manifested this world giving humankind the power to manifest beauty with each step and breath each of us takes on the Earth. You are a reflection of the creative force of the universe, and you have unlimited creative potential.

Along with your continued dreaming work, it is essential to explore and release the self-sabotaging beliefs that live so strongly within. For if you engage in the practices of dreaming without being aware of and releasing the self-sabotaging beliefs rooted in your unconscious, these beliefs override your desires and begin to destroy your work. If you fully engage your imagination while your unconscious tells you your practice will be unsuccessful, it is like driving with one foot on the accelerator and one foot on the brake at the same time. You will not be able to move forward. Your efforts will keep stalling out.

THE BELIEFS THAT BIND US

If I instructed you to go within and imagine what blocking attitudes and beliefs sabotage your efforts to create a positive life for yourself, I know you will come up with information. We can all intuit and imagine beliefs that prevent us from allowing our creativity to flow. What I have learned is that the seeds that created the strongest plants are the ones planted at a preverbal age. The seed might have been planted by your parents or another authority figure. It might not even be something that was said to you. It might have been a disapproving look that you observed when you got very excited about something you were doing. It might have even been a gesture that you misinterpreted as disapproval.

It could have been an attitude you picked up as you observed the behavior of others around you. Seeds of self-sabotaging beliefs blow in and take root in fertile ground when we are innocent and open.

Once the seed was planted, a pattern was created. The process of self-sabotage takes on a life of its own. Every time you begin to tap into your creative potential, this powerful unconscious belief comes through as if it has been your best friend all of your life and says, "Don't take the risk. Your plan is not going to work. You can't do it."

The purpose of this next journey is to discover a core blocking attitude or belief that is preventing you from tapping into and manifesting your true creative power. You will bring this question to a helping spirit you trust. Your power animal, guardian spirit, or teacher will look at your life from a different perspective, then from your vantage point. You might be completely blind about the beliefs that have been driving you. The beliefs and attitudes tend to be so old, and you might have absorbed them so deeply into your way of perceiving yourself, that you are too close to identify what needs to be released.

A helping spirit can identify and shed light on a very old core belief that you are unaware of. You might be completely surprised by what your helping spirit shares with you.

JOURNEY TO RECOGNIZE WHAT BLOCKS YOU

Visit a power animal or teacher and ask your helping spirit to share with you the core attitude, thought pattern, or belief that is blocking you from using your creative potential. What needs to be released? What needs to be weeded out of your inner landscape and your inner garden? This is a self-sabotaging thought that has followed you throughout your life. This belief has been running you. This belief has blocked your ability to use your creative gifts and talents. This attitude might have served you in coping with your life, but now it is time to remove the plant from your inner garden. Here are just a few examples:

"I do not deserve to have the best that life has to offer."

"I am not good, smart, or talented enough to create what I desire."

"I do not have the time or resources to be creative."

"I am not worthy."

"I cannot trust myself to know what is best for me."

"Others will be jealous of me if I become successful. I do not want to draw attention to myself."

"Nothing good ever happens to me."

"I should not allow myself to dream too big. If I do I will fail."

"I am unlovable."

"I am undesirable."

"It is impossible for me to create my dream."

"I am obligated to follow the wishes of my family and not get distracted by my dreams."

When you return from this journey, take some time to reflect on what was shown to you. You might need some time to shed tears and grieve once such a powerful blocking belief is revealed to you. Or you might feel a sense of freedom as you finally understand how your creative efforts have been continuously blocked. As this information might be new and unexpected, take some time sit with the new awareness you have gained.

Obviously this is a journey you can repeat over time. It is like peeling the layers of an onion. A blocking attitude might have established itself at a preverbal age. To this core blocking belief, others might have been added as you grew up and took on beliefs from others and the society that has shaped you.

CEREMONIAL WORK TO RELEASE AND TRANSFORM YOUR OBSTACLES

It is not enough to simply discover the core attitude, thought patterns, and beliefs that are blocking you. You need to take action on this information. It is time to remove the plants and roots from your inner garden. I encourage people to perform a ceremony to release a blocking attitude or belief. Ceremonies have been used in shamanic cultures since the beginning of time to create change. You might wish to review the steps of creating a ceremony that I wrote about in chapter 1.

The intention here is to design a ceremony to release an internal belief that is blocking your creative nature. Always work with the spirit of love. You are taking a loving action toward yourself when you release what binds you. If you feel you need more guidance on a ceremony to use, you can journey to a helping spirit to get a suggestion for a simple ceremony to perform. There are a variety of ways to release what binds you to an old way of perceiving yourself. Try some different ways to work and notice what method holds the greatest power for you. I will give you some examples of ceremonies that you can work with. Use your imagination to adapt what I share to design a ceremony that feels right to you. While I like to use fire for releasing blocking attitudes and beliefs, if fire is not an element you feel drawn to work with, find another element that calls to you. Find an element that you would prefer to work with, which feels like an ally for you. Start with your preparation, perform your ceremony, and close by giving thanks.

Many of my clients and students prefer to do simple and small ceremonies. In this way they can start wherever they are without feeling a lot of pressure to create a big ceremony that might feel overwhelming at first. No matter how simple your ceremony is, you want to create it in a sacred way. This is where the power lies.

Fire Ceremony

I love to lead fire ceremonies. Fire is the great teacher of transformation and transmutation. Fire takes from us what needs to be released and transmutes the energy.

Make a tangible object that can be burned. You can create a talisman or power object that holds the power of your belief, which you can release into the flames. You can find a stick as you walk in nature while focusing on what you wish to release. Take some yarn and unwind from your psyche your self-sabotaging belief while you wind its power onto the stick. You can make an object that comes from remnants of plants and trees that you can use to create your talisman. Take some time to make sure you have not just made a representation of your blocking belief. Sing, blow, dance, drum, or rattle the power of the blocking belief into your talisman so it embodies the power of what you are releasing.

There are a variety ways to perform a fire ceremony. If you do want to perform an outdoor fire ceremony, make sure it is safe to do so without creating destruction. A designated campsite is a great place for an outdoor fire. Or maybe there is a place outside of your house where you can safely build a fire with intention, as it is important to honor current climate conditions. You can also build a fire in an indoor fireplace. If you are limited in safe ways to work with fire, you can use the flame of a candle. Write the belief you are releasing on a piece of paper and burn it in a bowl or in a sink.

You are working in partnership with the spirit of fire to heal this core attitude or belief that you are releasing. As you build the fire, share with it your intention. When you perform a fire ceremony, you are working in partnership with all the elements. The wood used is earth. Fire needs air and some moisture in order to regulate the combustion. Earth, air, water, and fire combine together as one force participating in your healing.

You can offer to the fire your talisman or even a blocking belief you have written down on a piece of paper. Focus on what you are going to release. Feel it in your body. Once you feel ready, release it into the flame. Release the talisman into the fire while giving thanks and gratitude to fire as it works in your behalf to consume and transform your belief into pure divine energy. You might give an offering to the fire as it takes your blocking belief from you to be healed. I use cedar as an offering in the fire ceremonies I perform.

When your ceremony is complete, give thanks to the earth, air, water, and fire for participating in your ceremony. This work leads to an initiation and opens a new doorway for how you live your life. Give thanks to all the helping spirits you called in who witnessed you as you have taken a step forward in creating a positive life for yourself. Give thanks to yourself for finding the courage to engage in this powerful work.

You can invite friends and members of your community to participate in a fire ceremony. If they do not journey, simply ask them to imagine a blocking belief that needs to be released. The universe will answer the call to help release what truly needs to be transformed and healed. Share with them how to make a talisman or power object they can burn in the fire. Each friend can drum or rattle or hold the space in silence while one of you releases your talisman into the fire. There is an exponential energy that is raised when working with others in community.

WATER CEREMONY

You can perform a ceremony with water and create a talisman out of objects you find in nature that you can release into the water. This talisman holds the power of the belief. You can create a little boat out of sticks and plants, letting your belief sail away into the realm of spirit. Give thanks to water as your belief is released and transformed.

BUBBLE CEREMONY

A ceremony that will fill you with a childlike state of joy is to go outside with a bottle of bubbles. Hold your intention and blow bubbles into the air unburdening yourself from a blocking thought. Give thanks to air as the wind carries your blocking belief to the creative forces of the universe where it is transformed into love and light.

BURIAL CEREMONY

You can also write something down or create something out of nature that you can bury into the earth. In this way you can perform a funeral for letting go of what has been blocking you in life. Just remember to bury your belief with love. You do not want to bury negativity into the earth. You are releasing what binds you while at the same time transforming the energy of the belief into love and light.

BREAKING AWAY CEREMONY

You can find a stick in nature and while holding it, focus on the self-sabotaging belief you wish to be unburdened from. Break the stick as you release your connection to this belief. This is a symbolic act of disconnecting from an unwanted energy. Use your imagination to design a simple ceremony that feels right to perform.

DISMEMBERMENT JOURNEY CEREMONY

Another way that you can release something that is binding you is to perform a dismemberment journey where you ask a power animal, guardian spirit, or teacher to dismember your thought forms that sabotage your creative potential.

JOURNEY FOR DISMEMBERING A THOUGHT FORM

Bring your blocking belief, attitude, or thought patterns to a helping spirit and ask this spirit to perform a dismemberment ceremony. Your helping spirit will dismember this thought pattern to unburden you so that you are freed from your conditioned past, opening you up to your unlimited power and creativity.

When you feel that this journey is complete, return. Notice if you feel lighter after this burden has been dismembered and removed.

As with all the practices presented in *Walking in Light,* I will encourage you to be persistent with the ongoing work of releasing your obstacles. You will find that some old beliefs are easier to release than others. There are times when you perform a ceremony to let go of a blocking attitude that on an unconscious level your psyche is now ready to let go of. And you might feel an immediate release and new regained freedom. There are times when more work needs to be done to prepare your psyche for truly letting go of a belief that you have been carrying. Many of us want to be unburdened magically of all that is blocking us. To reap the rewards of the work, you need to be persistent and make a commitment to work through old issues still in need of healing.

Robert had been dealing with recurring health issues. He made changes in his lifestyle that would support his state of health. He was very attracted to the practice of shamanism and discovering how he could work spiritually to heal himself. At first he was excited about pursuing the practice of dreaming a healthy body into being. But shortly after beginning the work, he realized that he did not believe that he had the capacity to be successful at the work. He journeyed to discover his blocking belief. From a young age he was constantly told that he could not follow instructions and would never be successful at anything in life.

This belief followed him through life, and he always questioned his abilities. In reality Robert was a very kind, funny, and creative person. People loved being around him. But Robert had a hard time being with himself. He simply did not trust his own abilities. He put unreasonable expectations on himself, and this was certainly one cause of his weakened immune system.

Robert had some shamanic healing work performed on his behalf. He also understood well that he had more personal work to do to find a long-term solution for his healing. He continued to journey to look at his blocking beliefs. He performed a simple ceremony whenever a blocking belief came up for him. He wrote the belief he wished to release on a piece of paper and placed it in a sacred ceremonial bowl that he used for his spiritual work. He would then burn the paper in fire. He knew that due to the long-term nature of his health problems that there were layers of issues to work through and that performing one fire ceremony would not complete his work.

Robert worked at a good pace where he would do some releasing work and then let his psyche integrate what he had done before moving on to explore other issues. He felt a deep state of relief and peace every time he burned one of his blocking beliefs. Robert would feel free from a belief that was anchoring him to his past. Over time his health improved. He felt more confident in his dreaming work. He let go of blaming himself that he had created his illness. Robert came to understand the gift and all the teachings that his illness brought to his journey of discovering how to manifest his creative potential in a positive and healthy way.

Ultimately, you want to have the physical sensation in your body that the belief—the core attitude—has actually been released. You also want to watch the results of your work over time. Notice if your process of doing your dreaming work flows more gracefully and feels more empowered. Observe if you find a greater sense of excitement in designing a life that has passion and meaning for you. Notice if your self-confidence in your creative abilities gets stronger over time. Continue your practice to release self-sabotaging beliefs and attitudes as you continue to engage in your dreaming work. You will find that as you repeat practices to unburden yourself of blocking beliefs, the energy, power, and momentum of your dreaming work increases.

PART 5

EMPOWERING INNER EXPRESSION

CLOSE YOUR EYES AND GET COMFORTABLE. Take a few deep, cleansing breaths. As you breathe deeply, let any distracting thoughts dissolve or float away. Bring yourself into the present moment. Notice how you are feeling right now. This is a time out of your ordinary life when you can take an inventory of how you are feeling.

As you breathe, feel your heart. Feel your appreciation for life and acknowledge how precious life is. As you breathe deeply, allow love to soak in and flow through your cells. Remember how much love went into your creation, and let that love radiate through you into the world.

With your imagination, travel within to examine, experience, and observe how your inner garden is coming along. You have been planting seeds and also removing old plants that no longer serve you. You have been cultivating the soil. Run your fingers through the soil and feel if it is moist, soft, and rich. As a proud gardener would, observe your garden filled with beautiful and strong plants. Notice if any changes need to be made—don't judge, just observe. Acknowledge all that you have done to create a garden that will produce vital plants, flowers, and fruits. Your garden is a reflection of all the brilliant work you have done.

As you acknowledge the progress of your garden, as a caretaker, feed your garden with love. Remember that growth is a process. All life grows toward the light. Return from your garden and return to your heart. Again, breathing deeply, connect your heartbeat with the heartbeat of the Earth. We are nature and part of nature. The more you can connect with the heartbeat of the Earth, the more alignment you will feel with the cycles and rhythm of nature. You will be able to flow with grace and ease down the river of life through both the smooth and turbulent times.

Give thanks to your helping spirits for once again guiding you in your work. Give thanks to your ancestors who gave you life and give thanks for their continued support. Take a deep breath, and bring your awareness back into the room that you are in. It is now time to continue the exploration of new practices that will enrich your inner landscape.

11

The Unseen Power of
Your Thoughts and Emotions

A METAPHOR TO FOCUS ON as you continue your work is *what you feed grows*. In practicing a shamanic way of life, we attend to our behavior in the physical world, but we are also diligent in being observant about our behavior in the invisible worlds.

We were born to experience an entire range of emotions. It is our destiny to experience bliss and sadness, joy as well as depression, and love as well as anger. It is healthy for us to have a wide range of emotions; this is part of the experience of being human. Having emotions goes along with being passionate about life and how we fully engage in it. Repressing emotions creates stagnant energy, which leads to both emotional and physical illness.

In native cultures it is understood that there is a difference between expressing a thought or emotion that arises and sending out the energy behind that emotion. I knew a woman who was diagnosed with stomach cancer. She decided not to seek out Western medical treatment. Instead she traveled to South America to work with a shaman, who began his work by performing a diagnostic journey. With shamanic healing the shaman diagnoses the spiritual aspect of the illness. After performing the diagnostic work the shaman shared, "Someone sent you anger." The shaman went on to explain that the anger had created a spiritual intrusion or blockage in her body that created her illness.

When we look at the spiritual cause of personal and collective illness, the diagnosis of someone being sent anger is not uncommon. In shamanic traditions the difference between *having* an emotion and *expressing* our emotions versus *sending* the energy associated with an emotion is understood.

A CORE CHALLENGE
IN WORKING WITH EMOTIONS

There is often confusion when I teach the difference between expressing and sending energy. I had a dream one night that might help to clarify the difference. My dream shows the power of our invisible interactions. It shows how when we observe the behavior of others, they might not seem to be hostile. They might even have a smile on their face. But behind the smile, there is another scenario going on. There is an invisible level of interaction and communication between ourselves and others that we tend to ignore.

In my dream I was in an office. There was a group of co-workers gathered around a water cooler. It was a break time, and people were standing around drinking their coffee and tea together. The conversations seemed quite cordial. Then I became aware that some of the workers were sending invisible psychic punches to others. In the dream I would say to someone being psychically punched, "Are you okay?" Then I would say to another worker, "Did you see what you just did?" People were oblivious to what was happening on an invisible level. They were completely unconscious of the behavior that they were exhibiting toward each other. On the outside they were smiling at each other. Something entirely different was occurring on an unseen level.

If you reflect on vocabulary that we use, you can understand the point I am making. It is common to hear people complain and make statements such as:

"My partner is invading my space."

"I was kicked when I was down."

"I felt as if I had been stabbed in the back."

"I felt like I was shot down by my boss."

"I beat myself up after the argument with my lover."

"I felt like I was held hostage during the meeting."

"The room was filled with explosive energy."

"The energy was so thick you could cut it with a knife."

"I felt as if I had been beaten down, battered, bruised, or used as a punching bag during my interaction and by the words used."

"I felt like I was slapped across the face when my co-worker responded to me."

"I felt contaminated by the poisonous energy in the room."

I am sure you can come up with your own examples of feeling as if you were kicked, stabbed, shot down, pushed, shoved, beaten, bruised, and so on while engaging with another person or in a group. You might remember experiencing invasive energies. People often describe being under psychic or verbal attack. We often use violent terms when we describe our interactions with others. You know what it feels like to be in a room that is filled with anger. The feeling of that kind of anger is tangible. It does not feel good to be in that space. Oftentimes you want to leave as quickly as you can.

From a shamanic perspective, in looking at invisible energies exhibited during ordinary interactions, you were indeed pushed, kicked, stabbed, shot, invaded, or held hostage. There were poisonous energies *sent* out into the collective, which could create an immediate feeling of illness after such an interaction.

TRANSFORMING THE ENERGY OF AN EMOTION

Again *having* and *expressing* emotions are part of being alive. You have a right to feel anger based on people's behavior toward you and the collective at large. You want to experience the power of the anger or any other emotion. You can use the energy of your anger to fuel the good work that you do to be in service to others and the world at large. At the same time the spiritual work you need to engage in is to transform the energy behind the emotion. You want to transmute the energy behind your anger or other emotion to energy filled with light and love that feeds you and the rest of life.

Remember, what you feed grows. We create an impact on our communities through our psychic interactions. You need to be conscious of what you are radiating into the world while at the same time acknowledging the depth and wealth of feelings that go along with being human. In our culture we tend to *react* quickly to everything coming at us. It is important to stop and express your feelings when triggered without pulling the trigger. Otherwise you end up shooting an unwanted psychic dart or arrow to yourself, to others, and into the collective.

I started to explore this topic in the early 1990s. One day I was very irritated about the behavior of one of my friends. We had gotten into a heated discussion about a harmful action she was taking in behalf of another. We both kept the lid on the anger during our conversation. I left my friend's house, and I was processing our conversation while I was driving. As my attention was focused on the road, I heard my teacher Isis whisper in my ear, "What was that thought, and where did you just send it?" I thought about that statement. At that moment I realized that I had sent my unexpressed anger to my friend.

This realization woke me up to how unconscious we are in our culture when it comes to the impact of our psychic interactions. I used to experience this at peace rallies. People would be chanting for peace while radiating so much anger that they were feeding the power of hate, war, and separation. We have to evolve to a place of becoming aware of our invisible interactions with others. We must align our energies to feed the energies we want to manifest for ourselves and for the rest of life.

METHODS TO TRANSMUTE ENERGY

There are many simple methods you can use to transmute and transform the energy behind your thoughts and emotions. The methods I share might stimulate your imagination so that you discover some of your own unique ways to work.

We often behave in a habitual fashion. How we send energy oftentimes has simply become an unconscious habit that must be broken and replaced with a healthier way of expressing ourselves in the world. You might find at first that it is difficult to maintain your transmutation practice throughout the day. Have patience with yourself. You have to start somewhere. You begin by building up a level of concentration that raises your awareness to how you behave on unseen levels. Then you begin practices to shift your behavior. As these practices are continued, they start to become a way of life. Over time you will start to strengthen and build up your spiritual muscles. In the beginning you must put in some effort.

I once complained to my guardian spirit, "I don't think I'm getting this fast enough." My guardian spirit responded by saying. "What else do you have to do with your life?" Do not judge yourself or your timing. When you judge yourself, you run the risk of sending unwanted energies to yourself.

RECALL YOUR CORE INTENTIONS

When you feel triggered, take a step back from the situation. Take a deep breath and start to work with the energy behind your emotion. Don't repress your feelings. Experience fully what you are feeling. State an intention that you wish to transform the energy behind your thought or feeling to energy filled with love and light. In this way you radiate love to yourself and into the world. You want to feed your inner landscape with loving-kindness. And you also want to radiate loving-kindness into the world.

Make a Decree

Over my years of practice, I have found that working with a decree adds power and life to my intention. Try expressing different wording and notice what statements hold more power for you. You can phrase a decree by starting with the words *thank you*. As I wrote in chapter 6, by starting your decree with the words *thank you*, you acknowledge that the help you seek is already being given. You can also use a petition where you ask for help. When I get triggered, I simply state the following: "This is how I'm feeling right now. I have a right to what I'm feeling. Thank you for transmuting and transforming the energy behind my emotion to love and light that radiates into the world."

Breathing Is Transformative

Breathing deeply is a potent way to transform what is triggering you. When you get triggered, you might start to take fast and shallow breaths. If you stop, call a time out, and take some deep breaths, you will find that your state of consciousness naturally transforms. Take a few deep breaths and focus on your heart. It is usually your mind that is in a state of reaction. When you can breathe and focus on your heart, you will find that your energy dramatically shifts and transforms. You will shift out of a reactive state. Once you are in a calmer state, you can continue to work through your current emotions. Breathing deeply will also help you to transmute the energy that you are sending.

Impose Something You Love on the Situation

If a strong reaction is evoked, think of a loved one and impose his or her image onto the face of the person that you feel challenged by. For example, you might impose the face of a baby, kitten, puppy, your favorite flower, or a beautiful place in nature. What thoughts, what kind of energy do you want to send to those very precious beings that you love?

I love kittens, and I adore elephants. When I am angry with someone, I immediately impose the face of a kitten or elephant onto the person I am triggered by. I don't want to send unwanted energy to a being that I adore and that I wish to protect from harm. I am sure you feel the same.

RECALL WHAT YOU ARE GRATEFUL FOR

When you are in a reactive state, stop and reflect on what you are grateful for. Remember simple things about life that you love, such as the first time you ate ice cream, your favorite dessert, cherries, or when you first saw the ocean or snow. You might reflect on how grateful you are for the beauty of the sunrise, sunset, or the night sky. This will create a sense of calmness where you can express and work through your current emotions.

REDIRECT WITH YOUR SENSES

You can carry a small bottle of your favorite organic essence such as rose or lavender oil. Smelling the beauty of the fragrance will help you to stop your reaction and transmute the energy you are sending. When triggered, you can also take a sip of water. As you drink, reflect on what energies you are sending into the water. This will also help you to stop your reaction. Listen to the sounds of children laughing or the birds singing.

TURN TOWARD WORDS THAT INSPIRE YOU

You can carry notes of words or phrases in your pocket that are filled with love and inspiration. When you are triggered, you can read these words or phrases. Examples of inspirational phrases are:

All is in perfect order.

I am open to the gift of life.

I am held in the loving arms of the universe.

I shine as brightly as the stars above.

I am in my divine perfection right now.

I choose peace, love, and light.

I choose to focus on the good in life.

CALL UPON THE ELEMENTS FOR HELP

You worked with nature as a healing force. Working with the elements can assist your transmutation practice.

You can use water to wash away a challenging state. Wash your hands while visualizing or feeling the negative energy flowing from you and being transformed into light.

You can stand in the wind and imagine the wind carrying away what needs to be released and transformed. You can blow bubbles in the wind releasing a challenging emotion.

Light a candle. Imagine the flame transmuting your intense feelings into what you want them to be.

You can bury your troubles in the earth. Don't just toss them into the earth. Rather hold the intention of transforming the energy into love.

Mark has a very high-pressure job at a successful company. He finds that due to the pressure of his job as well as the business interactions he engages in, he easily moves into states of anger and frustration. Mark started to take frequent breaks and go into the restroom. He turned on the faucet and washed his hands while focusing on his intention to shift the energy he was radiating. The water would feel calming to him, so he could relax and breathe deeply. He would feel a lighter state of being as the water would take from him the energy of his anger and frustration. The more Mark did this, the easier he found it to experience the energy behind his emotions as an energy filled with love and light. This positive behavior became a habit.

BEING CONSCIOUS OF YOUR PART IN THE WEB

In the practice of shamanism it is taught that our behavior affects all in the web of life. What we do to one part of the web of life affects all. This is classic and "old time" shamanic understanding. You have experienced how the practice of shamanism embraces unity consciousness. Using the principle of unity consciousness when you send a thought or energy to somebody who you are angry with, you are also sending that energy to yourself, to a being that you love, and to all of life.

Jessica shared with me that she worked in an office where she had frequent conflicts with her co-workers. The energy in the office felt dense, and she often found herself feeling like her stomach was in a knot. She began breathing deeply while focusing on her heart when the energy felt dense in the office. Jessica reported to me how often a conflict would stop midsentence as she would do this. She could really feel how her lack of reaction would change the dynamics of the behavior between herself and a co-worker. Jessica started to feel safer at work and more relaxed. She found she could breathe easier and did not have to concentrate so hard on breathing deeply and through her heart. By doing so, the energy lightened up in her office, and it became a healthier place for her to work.

HAVE PATIENCE WITH
YOURSELF AS YOU REFLECT

Over time you will find that although you still get triggered, the intensity of your reactions diminishes. There will also be times when you can catch yourself and stop and do your work. And there will be situations where you feel you ended up sending toxic energy to another and into the collective. At the end of the day you can reflect on what occurred. You always have the opportunity to do some further healing work and go back to the situation and clean up the energy that you sent.

Margaret went to a family dinner. Although she had gained confidence in her transmutation work, she was surprised when she was confronted with the old dynamics of her family system. She found herself becoming quite angered during a conversation with her sisters. She let her anger out and felt she had reverted to a young age when she would fight daily with her siblings.

When she came home, she sat on her couch and drank a cup of herbal tea. As she held the hot cup she closed her eyes and calmly reflected on her behavior. She let go of the guilt about how she should have behaved. She simply observed the scene from earlier on in the evening. With intention she asked her helping spirit if she could go back and "clean up" the energy she had sent and also left in the room. With her teacher, she traveled back to her parents' house. Margaret was able to travel back to the time of the dinner. She was able to now radiate love and light to her family. And with the help of her teacher, she transformed the energy she had left in the room.

We are all evolving together. There will be days when you find that your practice goes so smoothly. You will feel proud that you were able to hold the light, feeding yourself and the planet with love. And then there will be days where every single tool you have learned and tried does not work. This is okay and something you need to learn to accept. In those times, don't resist, and simply observe. The practice of observation is a powerful way to practice transmutation, for when we resist a feeling or a thought, we end up fueling it. When we simply observe an emotion or thought, it will naturally change without a need to force a change.

At the end of the day accept yourself and acknowledge that you did the best you could. We sometimes put unrealistic expectations on ourselves. You are learning and growing. As my power animal says,

"What else do you have to do with your life?" Set your intention to remember that tomorrow is a new day. You will have new opportunities to put into action the spiritual practices you are working with. As you build up your spiritual muscles, the work will require much less effort over time. You will experience an inner peace and sense of well-being as "spiritual endorphins" are released into your body increasing your desire to keep up your spiritual work. Take time to reflect on the positive transformation that occurs as you continue your practice.

ALL ENERGY IS NEUTRAL

When I teach the practice of transmutation, a typical philosophical argument arises. For in the transcendent realms, there is no such concept of positive or negative energy. Through the eyes of spirit all energy is seen as neutral.

When you step out of the world of duality and move into a realm of oneness, it is true that all energy is neutral. At the same time, we live in a world of form. In the practice of shamanism it is clearly taught that *thoughts are things.* The esoteric teaching that all energy is neutral does not make it okay to behave in a mean-spirited fashion. It does not make it okay to rage drive and shoot psychic arrows at yourself or into the collective.

I do believe it is important for each of us to become responsible for and aware of how we behave in the non-ordinary, invisible, unseen, and psychic realms. The key is to learn how to express how we are feeling, transmute the energy behind the emotion, and be a vessel of love. When you act with loving-kindness, you can evolve into working with the teaching that all energy is neutral. And this is a powerful path in itself. For when you can truly perceive that all energy is neutral, you can absorb any energy that is in the collective and use it as fuel. Journeying on the subject of transmutation will give you further understanding and a perspective from the helpings spirits.

JOURNEY TO DISCOVER AND WORK WITH WHAT YOU RADIATE TO OTHERS

Visit a guardian spirit, power animal, teacher, or nature being you would like to consult with. Ask your helping spirit to show you in the invisible worlds how the energy of your thoughts and emotions is sent to others. Ask to be shown the impact on yourself and also on the collective. Ask for a very simple method of transmutation that you can try when you are feeling triggered by an event, a situation, or a person in your life.

For this first journey explore and discover something that you can work with so that at the end of your process, you feed the positive heart of the world. You do not want to feed the energies of hate and divisiveness. You wish to feed life with love that radiates to yourself and the planet, bringing harmony, balance, and good health to all. You might find that you need to do this journey from time to time to learn different methods for transmuting energy.

When you have gained the knowledge you are seeking, return to the room you are journeying in.

POSITIVE ENERGY IS CONTAGIOUS

We live in an environment that many perceive as toxic. We have acted in a way that does not honor the elements that sustain us. We have poured pollutants into the environment. One can say the same about what we pour psychically into the environment. From a spiritual perspective our outer world is reflecting back to us the toxicity of our inner environment.

Just like we need to change our behavior and clean up our outer environment, we need to do housecleaning on our inner world too. Alchemy is a spiritual practice that focuses on transmutation. One definition of the word *alchemy* is "working within and through the dense darkness inside." In the study of alchemy it is taught that we are all seeds of golden light. And it is important to do the personal work of transforming dark states of consciousness into states filled with golden light. When engaging in your personal transmutation practices, you create healing for yourself. But as the outer world reflects back your inner world, you also ultimately create healing for the planet and all of life.

Once comfortable with your personal practice to transform the energy behind your emotions and thoughts, you might focus on bringing your transmutation practice into the public arena. Energy is contagious. When good energy abounds, it lifts people higher. When the collective field of energy is dark and dense, it brings everyone down. It is like being in a weather system where everyone is impacted by the change in barometric pressure.

One late afternoon I went shopping at the grocery store. The day had been a long one, and I was not feeling well. I felt irritated by how long all the lines were at the checkout counter. I picked a line to stand in, and it felt like I would be there forever. I just wanted to go home. It seemed like everyone in line with me was having a bad day; everyone had a look of frustration on their face.

The woman who was working behind the counter had an immense smile on her face. She started talking to all the customers and in a loud voice asked each person how they were doing. She laughed and chatted, and she said something kind to each person. Suddenly I was smiling. And I then started to talk to the woman behind me. The other people in line also started smiling, and before we knew it, there was friendly conversation going on among everyone. Time sped up and my wait in line ended up being a pleasant one. I left the store with my groceries and a smile on my face.

I receive my mail at a post office box. One day I got my mail out of the box and was reading it at a counter by the window in the post office. There was a man standing next to me who looked sad. I started a conversation with him. And before I knew it, a sparkle returned to his eyes. When I said goodbye to him, as I was leaving, he looked me in the eye and said, "Thank you for brightening my day." This sincere statement of gratitude reverberated throughout me in a positive way for the rest of my day.

You can bring in your practice of transforming the energy at work, gatherings, meetings, or any place in public. When you find yourself in line or in a room where the energy seems dense, start smiling. Chat with people and uplift them by your presence. By brightening up someone's day, you might help them to transform what they are dreaming into being. You will feel so good every time your presence transforms the energy of others.

You can also shift the energy by working with your intention to transform the energy in the room to energy filled with love and light. You will want to continue this practice as you will feel fed with "spiritual endorphins" that produce the sensation of light and love flowing through you. In this way you begin to heal by your presence, which is how all the great shamans heal others and their communities. Lift people up by being a presence of love and light. There are rewards from smiling and making others smile too. This is a form of community service that becomes contagious.

NURTURING YOUR THOUGHTS THROUGHOUT THE DAY

As you look at the invisible energy of what you send out into the world, you also have to look at your thoughts that arise throughout the day. You must align your thoughts with a desired outcome. For example, let's say you want to manifest a wonderful relationship in your life, a community, a good job, or perfect health. Yet if you continue to repeat to yourself, "I can never have what I desire" or "I don't deserve the best that life has to offer," you defeat your creative efforts.

In the previous chapter you worked with releasing blocking attitudes and beliefs. But you might also find yourself looping certain self-sabotaging and defeatist thoughts throughout the day that will not lead to your desired outcome. Remember in shamanic teachings, thoughts are things. When you think something, you are planting a seed in your inner garden. A thought of love will flourish in your inner garden. Every thought or seed creates something in the world. Your life is a garden.

In spiritual traditions it is understood that everything that exists in the physical world is first formed in the invisible realms. Your thoughts and your words create an invisible world of substance that becomes your fabric of reality. It is important to learn how to reweave a new fabric of reality. The old collective paradigms are no longer working. There are old paradigms that are dissolving that do not support the health of the planet and life on it. There is an unweaving and unraveling process happening. As with the dreaming practices, you also must learn how to align your daily thoughts and your words with your desired outcome. In this way you start to weave a new fabric of reality into being.

METHODS FOR ALIGNING YOUR THOUGHTS

For many it is a habit to feed the negative. It is easy and also is part of our comfort zone. It takes energy and intention to break a negative habit and replace it with a positive habit.

AWARENESS

Find ways to be aware of what you are thinking throughout the day. This is necessary to be aware of what you are daydreaming into manifest form. We often go on automatic with the thoughts and words we use. You might carry a rock in your pocket and every time you hold the rock ask yourself the question, what are you thinking about right now? I have taped notes in my car, "Express, don't send." I write phrases on Post-its and leave them in my office and around the house that ask, "What are you thinking about right now?" Every time I look at these notes, they remind me to be aware of the energies I am feeding.

REPHRASING THOUGHTS

We often use the phrase *train of thought*. A train goes to a station. Consider where your train of thought is taking you. If you want to arrive at a different station, you have to learn to be more conscious about observing and rephrasing your thoughts.

Jeannette asked me if I would meet with her. She found herself frustrated with some of her dreaming work. Jeannette found it was easier to fall back into old looping self-defeatist thoughts. It was so much easier for her to imagine failure than success. And she also found a strange sense of comfort in slipping back into an old way of thinking. We talked about how falling back into looping old thoughts was simply a habit. And although old habits might not be healthy for us, the familiarity brings about a sense of the known and a false sense of comfort.

We discussed how making changes in our lives requires us to take a risk. Sometimes it is easier to stay where we are than to face our fear of failure. And sometimes knowing that any action toward making a change might lead to failure keeps us choosing to stay in our comfort level to maintain our life at a status quo.

It was not easy for Jeannette to make a choice to find ways to raise her awareness of when she slipped into looping sabotaging thoughts and then replace them with a positive line of thought. But once she set her intention and made the choice to do so, her process became easier, and she did not have to continue to effort so much with the work. Jeannette finally came to realize that she was not willing to compromise to live a mediocre life. She wanted to give her all to creating a meaningful life.

If you observe your regular looping thoughts, you will notice that they often are defeatist. To shift your thinking, surround yourself at work and at home with notes and cues that raise your consciousness and awareness to your train of thought.[1]

Shamanism is a daily practice that requires discipline. You have to strengthen your psychic muscles. You have to use the power of concentration and focus to align your thoughts with your desired outcome. Working with changing your thoughts leads to positive changes in your life. The work gets easier as rephrasing your thoughts becomes a habit. The neural pathways in your brain will change and grow into a direction of supporting a new way of perceiving life. You will feel more empowered in your daily life. The story you tell yourself is how you live your life.

12

Everyday Empowerment *through* Words, Forgiveness, *and* Gratitude

THERE ARE DIFFERENT WAVES that you can choose to ride and surf in life. There is a part of the population that chooses to just survive and does not want to look at themselves and how their behavior impacts not just their own personal life but also that of the planet. And there are many who are choosing to change their lives and thrive by living a life filled with meaning, passion, and weaving daily spiritual practices into their lives. There are many waking up and becoming more conscious of their behavior toward themselves, others, and the planet. There is a quickening of evolution going on. And the times we live in are calling us to wake up out of the collective trance and to use our spiritual practices to empower ourselves and to live more consciously.

The Earth has been giving us a wake-up call. The alarm clock has been ringing. Some are turning off the alarm and are waking up while others continue to push the snooze button. I often wonder how loud the alarm has to get for more people to wake up and participate in making the necessary changes to sustain life. We are living in a time when we do have to consciously disconnect from the collective energies that embrace hate, fear, separation, power over, and greed.

My teacher Isis has shared, "If you have heard the alarm go off and you do your work, you can choose to ride a different wave." Isis shares that if you are living a conscious life, you do not have to go down with the collective. You can rise above some of the denser energies that are being fed by collective energies. As part of a global spiritual community, you can feed a harmonious and sustainable energy that creates a different wave to ride.

You might find yourself making certain shifts in consciousness and then suddenly you find yourself caught back up in collective energies that no longer serve you. There are tools that can assist you in making a choice to not fall back into the consensus trance and use your energy to create positive and life-affirming changes.

THE CREATIVE POWER OF WORDS

Our thoughts are made up of words. Words are powerful seeds. Just as people living in a shamanic culture understand the power of thoughts, they also understand the power behind their spoken words. Our words and thoughts form in the invisible realms and manifest in the physical. Words are vibration. The vibration behind the spoken word travels up through the unseen worlds and then returns as a physical manifestation.

Words are seeds that grow in your inner garden. You need to focus and be aware of how you speak about yourself, others, and the world. The phrase *abracadabra* is an Aramaic term. The Aramaic term is *abraq ad habra.* Literally this translates to "I will create as I speak." If as a child you remember saying *abracadabra,* you were creating as you spoke this phrase.

Shamans are masters of telling healing stories when they work with clients. They know the art of using words to tell healing stories. They are very conscious of the words they use so that they bless their clients, communities, and the planet. We unintentionally curse ourselves and others with our words, so you want to learn how to use your words as blessings.

The Navajo people use the phrase, "May you walk in beauty." Many years ago I met a Navajo elder at a conference. She was listening to my lecture on the power of our words and thoughts. At the end of the lecture she approached me, and we talked about the phrase, "May you walk in beauty." She shared with me that it means to always make sure your words bless whomever you are speaking to. This is a powerful reminder for all of us as we engage with others. We must use the words that act as "good medicine."

Once you find words that contain the power of what you wish to manifest, write them down. Incorporate these words into your daily vocabulary. In this way you empower your life. In my first journey on the power of words, my teacher presented me with the word *brilliance*. He asked me to watch the energy radiating from this word. He said that if I wanted this energy to manifest in my life, I must speak this word throughout the day. A few of the words I use are *radiance, sparkle, wonder, passion, inspiration, resilience,* and *hope.* Notice what words become your favorites, and use your favorite words in your daily life as a blessing for yourself and also as a blessing for the world. This is a way to empower yourself and others.

In the Celtic traditions people had a wealth of poetic decrees that were used as blessings. Here are two examples of blessings that I was gifted with at special times in my life:

May the fairies sing your dream song on the threads of each full moon, may the trees whisper your wishes on their swelling buds and birth in the passions of awakening dreams.

May magic wrap about you and may your dreams be danced among the stars and blossom throughout the year.

You can phrase simple sentences where you send out blessings to others. Here are just a few examples:

Blessings of love be yours.

Blessings of health be yours.

Blessing of abundance be yours.

Blessings of the sun and the power of strength be yours.

Blessings are surrounding you.

You can also phrase blessings as decrees such as:

May your life be filled with joy, success, good health,
and happiness.

May you always know how much you are loved.

May you be surrounded by the power, love, and light
of the helping spirits.

JOURNEY TO LEARN ABOUT THE POWER OF WORDS

A practice to focus on is being conscious of the power behind your
words. Journeying to examine the power of the words you use can
be quite enlightening. Imagine traveling into a beautiful place
in nature. Call in a helping spirit to assist you. Ask your helping
spirit for a teaching about the energy behind your words. Try stating some words out loud while in the journey and watch how the
vibration of your spoken words travels up into the universe and
returns as form. Practice words you love and also words that hold
a negative connotation. Simply notice the energy created. Notice
how the energy might shift depending on what your intention is.
Learn how the words you use create the story of your life.

Return from the journey when you feel complete.

FORGIVENESS BRINGS FREEDOM

Every shift in consciousness that we make ripples throughout the
entire web of life. There are many states of consciousness that need
to be worked through as we continue to feed a healthy web of life.
Another aspect of the everyday empowerment of a shamanic way of

life is exploring the power of forgiveness and how to release your unhealthy connections with others.

Please understand that forgiveness cannot be forced. As you continue to feel empowered by the movement happening from living a shamanic life, you will feel a desire to release those who anchor you to your past. You will begin to acknowledge how people in your past mirrored and reflected back to you personal issues that needed to be explored and healed. In time you will find yourself compelled to release and forgive the people in your life from your past who no longer mirror back to you the truth of who you are and who you have become. Trust your timing. You will know when it is time to break the cord that binds you to an identity that you no longer feel connected to. This will bring to you a state of freedom you have been yearning for. Because once you release those relationships, you can attract people and situations into your life that reflect back to you your new awareness and state of health.

In your ongoing work there is a series of journeys that you can perform to examine issues of forgiveness for the betrayals, disappointments, losses, grudges, and even harms caused by others or by you in the past. You might be hanging on to your past through blaming yourself or others. Because your past can anchor you and prevent you from moving forward to create a positive life for yourself, you must acknowledge and then let go of the weight of your past. These blocking states of consciousness and unhealthy connections no longer serve you. They need to be acknowledged and released. These states can prevent you from engaging in life to its fullest. Here are some things you can do:

You can bring a known issue to your helping spirit and ask for a suggestion of a healing ceremony you can perform.

You can also ask a helping spirit for advice on an issue that might be tying you to your past.

A helping spirit can also help you dismember a state of consciousness you wish to release.

You can simply ask your helping spirit for a healing.

I want to offer one particular journey that you can perform for releasing states of consciousness that prevent you from fully engaging in your life. Perform the work in small steps so that you can get the benefit of keeping your focus and concentration on each aspect of the work.

JOURNEY OF FORGIVENESS

Allow your inner wisdom to reveal to you the states of consciousness that need to be healed. Call upon a helping spirit to assist you in your exploration. Hold the intention to travel to a great cauldron of light.

Look at where you might feel betrayed by life. Who has betrayed you? Who has disappointed you? Observe that there are people who you need to forgive or life circumstances that occurred where you felt betrayed or disappointed by a community or by life itself. What energies would you like to clean up and transmute?

Look at where and to whom you might have directed hatred and anger. Have you betrayed anyone by your behavior? Do you need someone to forgive you? Do not forget to include yourself in this list. Self-forgiveness is extremely important.

Allow your inner spirit and your helping spirits to reveal to you the inner states of consciousness that need to be examined, acknowledged, and released. This is a time to be cleansed. Look at connections to people who you need to release. Break your connection with collective energies that no longer serve you so that you are now free to ride a different wave.

In your journey hold the intention to travel to a great cauldron of divine light. This cauldron might be in the Lower, Middle, or Upper World. Your intention will guide you. Acknowledge the connections you need to release, ties that need to be broken, betrayals, disappointments, who you need to forgive, and collective energies that you need to let go of. You can also place into the cauldron any beliefs or past events that will lead you to forgiving yourself. Then release what needs to be healed into this cauldron of light. As you release the inner states that need to be healed, you release them into the divine light that transmutes their power and energy into love.

You are now freed of energies that bind you to a denser energy of life. You are now free to ride a different wave. Return from this journey experiencing yourself lighter, unburdened, and free.

Claire wrote me after she read in my monthly column my suggestion to work with the Cauldron of Light. She had been having struggles at her job with one person in particular.

After reading the exercise she promptly ran upstairs to do some cleansing work. She loved the imagery of the cauldron, and the cleansing she did felt powerful. She woke up the next morning before her alarm clock went off. The first thought that spontaneously arose in her mind was very clear and included a beautiful image of the Cauldron of Love and Light. She remarked how this was a wonderful way to start her day. She acknowledged that there was more clearing work to do. But she was in such a state of deep gratitude as working with the cauldron of light provided so much healing for her.

You can empower your life by engaging in simple ceremonies such as those suggested in chapter 10 on overcoming obstacles. You can also perform a journey to clear and cleanse from your daily interactions with others and the collective at large.

GIVING THANKS BRINGS JOY AND HARMONY

To native peoples every day is a day of thanksgiving, and gratitude is shared. Gratitude is given to the life-giving spirits that sustain life. Gratitude is given as the sun rises each day. It is never assumed that the sun will rise each day. Sunlight is essential for life. Gratitude and appreciation is given to the earth, air, and water for sustaining life. The directions are honored including the above and below. The ancestors are honored with prayers of gratitude. Gratitude is given to the animals, plants, insects, reptiles, rocks, and so on—the spirit that lives in all things. Helping spirits are acknowledged and given gratitude. And most important gratitude is given for one's life.

Shamans teach that gratitude is key to living a life filled with joy and harmony. Giving thanks and appreciation is part of the everyday empowerment of a shamanic way of life. Gratitude helps to build a good foundation that leads to a positive life and a good path. If you wake up in the morning only focusing on the challenges you will face during the day, you end up feeding the energy of these challenges. You do not want to deny what is happening, instead you want to feed the energy of the possibility for goodness to come to you. Follow your train of thought and the energy that you want to put into motion by how you begin your day.

When you begin your day with gratitude, you create a strong foundation for positive experiences to build on throughout the day. Gratitude and appreciation return you to a state of awe and wonder, which creates excitement. Excitement is a vibrant energy that fuels your creativity and the power of your dreams. Gratitude fuels your love for life and helps you maintain hope. Remember that humor is a transformative force. Continue to plant seeds of love, light, humor, and gratitude in your inner garden, and watch what grows in your life.

Upon awakening, give gratitude for your life instead of focusing on the challenges ahead. And then start to honor and give gratitude and appreciation for all that sustains your life and touches your heart. Reflect on simple things you can be grateful for. Think of someone in your life you appreciate.

Ted went through a difficult divorce, and he felt he could not feel grateful for anything in his life. He woke up each morning feeling like the sun had left his life and that he only had stormy times ahead. When I asked him what he felt grateful for, he was at a loss for words. He looked at me with a blank stare. I asked him if he had a favorite food or if there was a good memory from his past feeding a sense of well-being from a happy time of his life.

I told him how in my times of depression, I would think about the first time I played in the snow, which was such a joyful event for me. And I told him how I loved eating ice cream, smelling the lovely fragrance of a rose, watching the soothing waves of the ocean, and listening to the sound of a river. I asked him if there was anything he could think of that inspired a sense of joy, comfort, and gratitude. He resisted wanting to think of anything he could be grateful for, and I did not push him. I asked him to go within and notice if anything emerged. I watched as his face brightened as he remembered the day his parents brought him a new puppy.

Ted did start to focus on the simple things that he could be grateful for. He did not deny his sense of grief and loss that came from separating from his wife, but he did agree to work with dropping into times when he could focus on the joys of life. Ted began to post notes around his house with words, phrases, and blessings that would change his current beliefs about what was possible to create in his life.

As with all the practices that go into empowering one's life, it took time for him to embrace the possibility of a positive future. In time his grief lessened, he worked on self-forgiveness, and he shifted his life into working toward his vision of what would create happiness. This all started with being grateful for the simple yet potent joys of life.

METHODS FOR EXPRESSING GRATITUDE

These are some of the ways people express gratitude, offered as examples that you can draw on to create your own rituals and method. These daily practices will shift your perception and will feed your ability to create positive outcomes for your day and your life.

Begin your day with gratitude practices instead of focusing on the challenges ahead.

Upon awakening close your eyes and state words of thanks to the earth, air, water, and the power of the sun for sustaining you.

Greet your helping spirits and thank them for their continued help and protection.

Give thanks for positive situations, helpful people, and all the beauty you will experience during the day.

Give thanks to your ancestors for the gift of life.

State your gratitude to the Spirit of the Land that holds you in love.

Give thanks for your life.

Visit your altar, and sit with the sacred objects and prayers you might have left on your altar to empower your life.

If you feel called to, leave an offering outside of your house giving thanks for the goodness that will come into your life today and give thanks for your life.

A friend of mine met a Tibetan nun in a bookstore in Santa Fe. The Tibetan nun had been imprisoned in China after her monastery was invaded. During her time in prison she had been tortured. The Tibetan nun was engaging in conversation with some people in the bookstore. Someone asked her how she healed herself, for everyone present could witness the love, light, and joy radiating through her. She said she healed herself by repeating the following mantra: "Thank you for everything. I have no complaints whatsoever."

This story is something to sit with and reflect on, for life is not out to get us. Life is always bringing something to us. We can transform our challenges with the power of gratitude.

13

Protection, Perception, and Projection

A COMMON QUESTION PEOPLE ASK IS, "How do I protect myself if somebody is sending energy toward me that is toxic or poisonous?" Please understand that you have a choice about whether you receive and absorb that kind of energy. My spirit teacher Isis explains this by using the metaphor of receiving a package in the mail. You always have the choice to write on the package "return to sender." You do not have to accept and receive the package. In shamanic traditions it is taught that you always want to make sure that you are radiating love. You already worked with the principle of what you send out comes back to you. Therefore, set your intention to "return to sender with love."

This is important work for anyone who is in a service profession or who works with the public. Some of the people I work with who struggle with health issues are people who are in a helping profession such as a psychotherapist, social worker, nurse, doctor, or lawyer. When clients are emoting, some form of protection is needed to avoid taking on the energies that are being sent into the room. The hope and vision, of course, is one day we will all become conscious of the impact of unseen energies, but until that day comes, we must take care of ourselves and make sure we are filled with power. If your profession keeps you in the public, there are a variety of ways to fill yourself up with power thereby creating a psychic boundary that cannot be permeated.

INVOKING POWERFUL PROTECTION

In the 1980s a Chumash medicine woman taught me to imagine seeing myself surrounded and protected by a translucent blue egg. I have in turn taught this to thousands of people who have benefited from working in this way. You can journey on a color that you can surround yourself with that will help you to create a boundary between your own psychic field and the field of the collective. You could also journey and ask for guidance on a protective symbol that you could visualize within that protects you from taking in unwanted energies.

A woman in one of my workshops felt she was being psychically attacked by a friend, and she asked me how to deal with the issue. We talked about it, and I shared some different tools she could work with. She was very fearful, and she kept talking to me about this issue throughout the day. That night I had a dream. The spiritual teacher Jesus appeared to me in a luminous state, and light was streaming through his hands. I received a telepathic message from him. Jesus said if you are filled up with light and allow that light to flow through you, there are no outside energies that can impact you in a negative way. When you are filled with light, harmful energies cannot enter into your psychic space. Keep working on experiencing your inner divine light to help you maintain your health as you engage with others.

As you continue to evolve and empower your life by living a shamanic life, you will begin to understand that other people and situations in your life act as mirrors that reflect back your inner state of consciousness. A powerful stance to take is to stop blaming others for attacking you, instead explore what is happening in your inner world. Be courageous and examine how those in the outer world are providing a mirror for you to look at your unconscious behavior. You might learn that you are also participating in behavior that seems attacking in nature. The more you can be honest with yourself and look at transforming your inner world, the more empowered and protected you will feel in life.

YOUR PERCEPTION CREATES YOUR REALITY

I am sure you have had the experience of being at a gathering, meeting, or party with others. One person might say the energy in the room is wonderful. And another might say that the energy feels dense and negative. Both people are in the same room among the same people, but each person has a different perception of the energy. You might also observe this when you eat out with others. One person enjoys a dish that another thinks is terrible; it is all in your perception. These are very simple examples to give you a sense of the teaching.

In life some people focus only on the suffering they perceive in others while others focus on the beauty and the joy of life. You can think about examples where you have seen how your perception creates your reality. The challenge is often to shift your perception in a world filled with so much change and dissolution.

Many of us look through the eyes of our conditioned mind and judge what we see around us. The conditioned mind was created by the seeds that society planted into our garden. Many of these seeds grew strong roots and plants and sculpt our beliefs about ourselves and the world around us.

We all experience challenges in life and, at the same time, if you lift the veil behind your challenges, there's an incredible beauty to life. Even when life seems dark and filled with grief and suffering, there is another level of fertile ground that transforms suffering into beauty. You have to train your mind to shift out of seeing the negative and only the challenges. You need to embrace the beauty that life has to offer and perceive the light and gifts in everything. As you continue your spiritual work, you will learn how to dig deeper in your inner garden to find the gold and perceive how rich life is with all the challenges and growth experiences. It is all a shift of perception.

METHODS FOR SHIFTING PERCEPTION

Do you react to what life brings to you? Do you learn from what life brings to you? Are you able to lift the veil and still experience the beauty of life no matter what is occurring in the outer world?

EXPRESS GRATITUDE

One key to shifting perception is learning how to improve your attitude. Appreciating life as you work with your gratitude practices helps to shift your perception. Learning how to live in a state of love, appreciation, and gratitude for your life empowers your life and creates deep transformation. As you learn how to focus on the beauty, your perception changes. As your perception changes, so does your life.

RECALL CHILDLIKE WONDER

Another way to shift your perception is to return to the state of awe and wonder that you held as a child. Remember back to your childhood to how everything seemed so new and fresh. This will assist you to perceive the beauty that life has to offer. This creates an excitement for life where you notice that your attitude changes. Life will keep bringing you a variety of experiences. As my teacher Isis always reminds me, "Life is an adventure."

SEE THE HUMOR IN LIFE

Humor plants wonderful seeds in your inner garden. Using humor is a great tool in learning how to shift your perception. Laugh at yourself. When you find yourself falling off the spiritual path, get up, brush yourself off, and get back on the path. Spiritual work is serious, but as you learn how to bring more humor into your life, you will find it to be a great healing force.

A core principle in spiritual teachings is that our outer world is a reflection of our inner state of consciousness. The esoteric teaching "as above, so below; as within, so without" is also a shamanic understanding. Changing your inner landscape transforms you, and your outer world will reflect those changes back to you. You will feel empowered in your daily life. You begin to be guided by spirit, instead of just following your ego. You start to ride a different wave of life than you have been riding before, and you begin to feel harmonious and peaceful inside. This creates healing for yourself and also in the world, for harmony within always creates harmony without.

You have been performing practices to raise awareness of the energy you send into the world. In chapter 12, I planted a seed within you by mentioning that all energy is neutral. If you believe and perceive that you live in a toxic environment, then you are living in a toxic environment. This means that you need to learn to shift your perception about what you take into your body. You do not want to absorb toxins or be afraid of the food you eat, the air you breathe, or the water you drink.

Just as you are divine light, everything around you is divine light too. You will find that a practice that adds to your health and well-being is learning how to absorb all that you take in as divine light. One day all people on the planet will honor the Earth and the elements that sustain us. Until that day comes we must learn how to transmute what we take in and absorb the light of life. Soak in the goodness of life. Here are some ways you can absorb the light of life:

When you eat your food, set your intention to absorb the light of what you eat.

Do the same as you drink water and breathe the air.

Absorb fully the light of the sun.

Absorb the power and the beauty of all the landscapes you walk through.

Most of all, transmute the energies that surround you and absorb the light to empower you on your life path.

PROJECTING OUR PERCEPTIONS

You are transforming the energy behind your emotions and thoughts so that you continue to feed your life and the world with love and light as well as rephrasing the thoughts you use throughout the day. You now have the knowledge that your thoughts end up creating stories that shape your life. Your thoughts are made up of words. You have direct experience with how potent words are in changing yourself and the world.

Now it is time to examine how you project onto others with your thoughts and words. As humans we project our perception onto others. I was teaching an ongoing workshop where participants would return every six months to continue their studies with me. At the beginning of our third session together, a participant walked up to me as I was preparing the space we were meeting in. She asked me if I was feeling okay and remarked that she had never seen me look so tired. I was actually not feeling tired. I was preoccupied with getting the room in order and setting up the altar for our circle. Suddenly I felt my energy drop. A true sense of fatigue settled in.

Then another participant entered into our meeting space. She walked up to me and exclaimed that she had never seen me look so healthy and strong. She said I looked radiant. You can imagine how my energy shifted upon hearing these words. I immediately perked up and felt wonderful.

While watching the news after a destructive catastrophe, we are flooded with images and reports showing the level of suffering of those affected. Your heart might feel like it is breaking open as you perceive so much destruction and suffering. I have come to realize that heart-break is actually an expansion of the heart. As my heart breaks, at the same time it opens, and I expand my capacity to be a vessel of love and light.

Projecting True Compassion, Not Pity

The issue is that during challenging times, many people start to project pity onto others. Pity is actually a burden. Imagine that a catastrophe happens in your life or you are going through some very challenging initiatory experience. Imagine that you can share your experience with many thousands or even millions of people. Would you want thousands of people sharing or even thinking, "You poor thing!" When others project pity, it is a heavy energy that sits on you that anchors you and makes it harder to mobilize your own energy to find creative solutions to whatever challenge you are facing. In challenging times I am sure you want people to be there for you, hold the space while you go through your journey, and cheer you on. If others project strength onto you and see you in your divine light, this creates energy that inspires and is uplifting.

If you want this for yourself, then you need to do this for others too. But in our culture when we feel compassion, we tend to misinterpret the power of compassion and we translate it into pity. Compassion is the feeling of empathy toward others. When we see others suffer, we often try to put ourselves in their situation, and we imagine how they might be feeling during a time of challenge. When we pity others, we project the energy of suffering onto them. This projects and sends defeatist energies to others. The key is to be compassionate toward others and while empathizing with them to open our hearts and hold them in love. Imagine others as having the inner strength to be successful at moving through any challenges they might be facing.

WHAT YOU FEED GROWS

The same is true when someone we care about shares a new creative idea or project. It is not uncommon to think or even say out loud, "That's crazy; he will never manifest that idea." Remember, what you feed grows. The more you nurture your projections of suffering, the more suffering grows. The more you nurture your projections in perceiving the beauty and what is working, you feed the energy of strength and beauty.

You must always stop and reflect on what you are projecting onto others. Are you projecting the best onto loved ones and people in the world? This does not mean you should deny the challenges that occur. But when you lift the veils between the worlds and look beyond human conditioning, you will see beauty, joy, love, and divine and perfect health.

Choosing Your Focus

Notice the difference in how you feel when you shift your perception in the following ways:

> When you are conversing with others, notice something that you can focus on that feeds the energy of their beauty and divine light.

> When you watch the news or read newspapers, focus on the courage, beauty, strength, and divine light of groups of people that the media is covering.

> When you look in the mirror, don't focus on how tired you look or how your age is showing. Focus on how beautiful you do look and the light shining out of your eyes.

Imagine what the results would be if you fed the strength of your loved ones, friends, and co-workers, and they fed your strengths too. Project the best onto yourself and also onto the world. Continue to reflect on your behavior. You want to exhibit compassion. Remember the phrase *may you walk in beauty,* and always project beauty and blessings onto yourself, your loved ones, and into the world.

SHIFTING YOUR CONCERN ABOUT PLANETARY CHANGES TO PROJECT LIGHT

Walking a spiritual path is not always easy. There are all kinds of obstructions to move out of the way. For the truth of the matter is that if we are truly on a spiritual path, we are driven by spirit and not by our personality and ego. When we focus only on the seen and visible world, it is so easy to fall off of our spiritual path. The collective and the conditioned mind is drawn and magnetized to the drama and trauma of what is occurring in the outer world.

It is a challenge to be so hypnotized by our conditioning. It can be a struggle for many to focus on the beauty that life has to offer instead of only perceiving the challenges. We are human beings with a personality, ego, mind, and body. And these aspects lead us to experiencing great joy and also experiencing states of suffering. For when we perceive the world through the eyes of ego, the world is not looking so good. Life is falling apart all around us. The climate is changing to such a degree that we are watching mass changes to the Earth impact not just humans but all of life. There are many challenges manifesting in politics and the economy, and the violent behavior of humans toward each other and the rest of life is not what we would like to see continue.

Then we do our spiritual work. And once we are in contact with our spirit, we leave the arena of duality and move into a place of oneness. From this place of divine light and love, everything looks different, for in the arena of spirit there is no judgment or imperfection. It is what it is, and spirit accepts the changes that are leading to evolution and growth.

Here lies the paradox. If you see the divinity in floods, drought, cyclones, war, abuse, and violence, do you just sit around passively and say that everything is in divine perfection, that you do not need to care, worry, or take any action? The answer to this question is no.

Human beings have not been taking care of the Earth, which is our home. Consider your own body. If you continue to put toxins into it and do not take care of it, at some point your health breaks down. When health does break down, it is important to take action and make changes to how you take care of your physical body. You need to learn how to work with your emotions and mental states so that you tend to your state of health, and most people find a tremendous amount of healing in adding spiritual practices to support their health and well-being. Taking care of body, mind, and spirit works together to create a harmonious life. Disharmony causes illness.

What we are seeing in our lifetime are the results of not taking care of ourselves, but also not taking care of the earth, air, and water that give us life. Not working through personal issues such as a desire for amassing more on the material level has created disharmony. We go into forests and jungles and cut down trees by the millions without honoring them or thinking about the web of life and how the life of these trees contribute to the health of the planet. We kill entire species for financial gain and not just dishonor their beauty and life but don't recognize how they contribute to the health of the web of life. And the list goes on.

Not working with egoic mental states has led to people becoming power hungry, causing violent behavior toward children, women, men, and all of life. The human race has not been spirit driven. So although we fall into places of despair, it is time for all us to stand up and do our spiritual work to shift our own consciousness and perception. It is time for us to stand together as a global community so that we can create exponential change, which leads to healing for the Earth and all of life.

And we need to accept that we might not see the physical manifestation of our efforts in our lifetime. At the same time it is important for us to surrender to the understanding that the Earth is evolving and that landscapes are changing as they have done since the beginning of time. We need to continue experiencing our divine light and perceive the beauty in life. We cannot stop this practice because we are troubled by world events. Spiritual work that is only performed while remaining attached to the outcome is not spiritual work. When we become attached to outcomes, it is the work of ego not spirit.

One day I was walking in my arroyo after a very intense day of work. I needed a way to de-stress and clear my mind. Walking the same path for twenty years and feeling my feet connecting deeply with the earth is healing balm. As I have shared with you I have received a wealth of omens and signs that have guided me on my path and also have reminded me of the power of the unseen and the magic of life by walking in nature. I can visit with my favorite trees that have become friends, gaze upon beautiful red crystalline rocks, and listen to the bird songs. The arroyo is not just a place for me to receive messages; it is also a place of comfort.

Santa Fe had been in a drought. As I was walking I could not help but start to worry about the dryness and the fate of this land. I got lost in thinking about the future and how long I would get to enjoy walking in this amazing and beautiful landscape. And then I brought myself back from feeding the challenge and hardship to appreciating all the gifts I receive from the land. I brought myself back into the present moment. In reality the trees looked healthy and vital. I was projecting suffering onto them. I had to shift my perception to see the divine health of the land. As I did this, a beautiful corn snake appeared on the path. That was a great omen for me.

There is a physical shift that I can feel as I shift my perception and see the divine health of all in the web of life and the Earth. When I perceive the health of the land versus the struggle, I feel my third eye opening. Shamans see with their strong eye, which in some spiritual traditions is called the third eye. This refers to your invisible eyes, which provide perception beyond ordinary sight. The strong eye is the gate that leads to the inner realms and spaces of higher consciousness. The third eye sits above your eyes in the middle of your forehead. When I use my invisible sight to perceive beyond what I am only seeing in the visible, all that I see shifts. It is like I have another set of eyes that see into the unseen rather than only what is visible to me. With this other set of eyes I see the strength in the trees, the plants, and all that is alive. And by seeing through my third eye, I can change what I am projecting.

In doing so I have felt myself surrender more to the divine intelligence of Nature. I feel in all my cells that the Spirit of Santa Fe knows what she is doing. I trust how she is allowing the land to be sculpted and changed. I don't understand on a rational level all that is occurring. But I have trust and faith in the process of evolution.

We do need to keep taking action to protect our environment, but we need to blend this with strengthening our spiritual work. A key part of our spiritual work is to keep our focus on the beauty and divine strength and light of all that is alive. Most of us continue to seesaw back and forth with being able to touch into the divine and then back into an egoic state of worry, fear, and anger.

METHODS FOR CHANGING
HOW YOU PERCEIVE THE WORLD

We know that the world is our projection. When you use your invisible sight to change the image of your projection, you end up changing your life and all connected to the web of life. Here are some ways to do this:

Carry words, inspirational phrases, and precious images with you to help shift your consciousness.

Daydream about the beauty of the world you wish to live in.

Bathe in these words, phrases, stories of success, and the beauty of life. Feed the energy of the words, phrases, and stories you wish to give life to.

If you cannot shift your awareness and perception during stressful times, then you need to ask yourself what benefit will come from your spiritual work. You cannot experience a spiritual state only when it is convenient for you to do so.

Use more of your invisible senses to shift your perception of what is happening for you and in the world. Focus on opening your invisible senses to project light onto the Earth and the world.

SEEING THE WORLD
THROUGH THE EYES OF SPIRIT

In Siberia and throughout Asia many shamans wear a mask and regalia of a helping spirit while doing their shamanic work. While wearing a mask imbued with the power of a helping spirit, they merge completely with the spirit, being able to see a client and the world through the eyes of spirit rather than through the eyes of ego.

To gain a greater understanding of using your unseen senses to shift your perception and projections, practice seeing the world through spirit eyes. You can do this by merging with a helping spirit and looking through its eyes. The spirits often perceive patterns of energy or illness as a lack of love or light. You might already have had the experience of merging with a helping spirit when you journey. This next journey will allow you to lift the veils of your ordinary world and see the world through the eyes of spirit.

JOURNEY TO SEE THROUGH THE EYES OF SPIRIT

After preparing for the journey, meet your teacher in human form. Ask your teacher if you can merge with him or her. Observe your life and the world around you through your teacher's eyes. Observe how a transcendent spirit views life. This journey will shift your perception and help you to understand what it means to see the world through the eyes of spirit.

When you have completed your journey, thank your teacher for the experience. Disengage from your teacher as your teacher returns to the transcendent realms and you return back into your room again.

Once back take some time to reflect on your experience. After completing this exercise consider any "corrections" you need to make in regard to your attitude about your life or about the state of the world.

LIVING *in the* FLOW *of the* SACRED

BEGIN BY TAKING A FEW DEEP BREATHS. Feel your breath flowing through your body. Breathe deeply. Experience your energy moving into your heart. Feel your heartbeat and let your heartbeat connect to the heartbeat of the Earth. Breathe deeply as you focus on something or someone very special to you in life, something very precious to you. As you experience what you love about life, something very simple, let your heart expand. Feel the energy flowing within as you breathe. Experience the power of love flowing within and without as you inhale and exhale. As you breathe deeply feel your connection with the Earth. The Earth is a living body that holds and nurtures you. You are more than your body and your thinking mind. Your body and mind are required to function in life as you perform daily activities. You are spirit. You are light. You are one with the power of universe.

As you continue to breathe deeply, go within and experience a flame of light growing inside. As you continue to breathe, this light grows, flows, and radiates throughout your cells. This process is effortless, for your true nature is light. Allow your light to radiate and flow. Sink into your light, and absorb the light into your cells. Experience it. As this light flows through you and radiates, allow it to shine filling the space that you are in and let it grow beyond that space out into the world. You do not have to learn about your inner spirit. It is about learning how to connect with it and learning how to live from it. This light is you; remember, this is the truth of who you are.

Now it is time to return. Return to experience the beautiful cloak of your body and the power of your mind that helps you navigate through life. Remember you are body, mind, and spirit flowing in a beautiful way with grace, passion for life, and hope. Experience your body with your breath, and experience your connection to the Earth. With intention, return to the room that you are in right now.

14

The Light Within

I SHARED IN CHAPTER 7 how shamans go through a series of dismemberments and initiations. The initiatory experiences of the shaman lead to a transition of dissolving ego to remember the truth of his or her spiritual identity. To experience a deep connection to unity consciousness and to the creator, dismemberment and initiation are important parts of empowering a shamanic way of life because ultimately we are light.

Light transforms and light heals. As we learn how to be a vessel of light and unconditional love, the world around us heals. It is important to continue your practice of experiencing yourself as *Source*. The more you experience your divine nature and light, the more you heal and become a stronger and more potent healing presence in the world.

Remember that this light is always flowing through you. You can create healing in the world by being a strong presence where you radiate light. This light flowing through you empowers you in your daily life.

Find a time in the day—in the morning before you rise or at night before you go to bed—when you can deepen your connection with your inner light on a daily basis. I put on my favorite expansive music, lie down, and journey within. Just as I offered you in the guided meditation that opened this part of the book, I experience my light flowing and being absorbed into my cells. I do this every day for just a few minutes. This practice allows the connection to my spiritual light to strengthen. This is a simple practice that creates profound healing and transformation.

TRANSFIGURATION THROUGH LIGHT

When I was writing *Medicine for the Earth,* I had a very powerful dream. The Egyptian god Anubis appeared and introduced himself to me. He then gave me a very short message. He told me that the practice of *transfiguration* was the missing piece of my work to heal the environment. I awoke the next morning curious about this message, for at the time I did not know what the word *transfiguration* meant. I learned that the word means shape shifting. I felt confused as I could not connect shape shifting to working with reversing environmental pollution.

Due to the wonderful conversations I had with Kathy, a client and friend of mine, I was able to understand the power of the practice of transfiguration. Kathy was dying of liver cancer. She was a fundamentalist Christian and out of desperation was willing to explore alternative ways of healing. I taught her how to journey, and she had profound journeys in her visits to Jesus who appeared as her teacher. One day Kathy and I were taking a time out from our work, and we were just chatting together as friends. When I shared with her my dream about Anubis and his message, Kathy became excited and animated as she shared with me one story after another recounting the miraculous healings that Jesus performed when he transfigured into a being of light. A light went off in me when she shared these stories. Of course, the power of light transforms.

I researched miraculous healings in different spiritual traditions including shamanism, and time and time again I read accounts of miraculous healings occurring when the shaman, healer, mystic, sage, or guru had transfigured into a bright radiant light. Many of my students shared with me visits to some shamans in Siberia and also in

Peru who taught that they heal their clients by radiating light. I felt that if mystics, shamans, and healers could use this practice to heal, we all have the ability to do the same, for light is our essential nature.

RADIATING DIVINE LIGHT IS OUR NATURE

When I teach people to transfigure and experience their divine light, some people get a bit confused. Some mistake the transfiguration process as an out-of-body experience, and they try to go out to meet the creator. As we are a reflection of the creator, light is who we are. There is nowhere to go to experience our radiance. We journey within to our true nature.

I also find that many labor too much in this process. People try so hard to *do* something. Using the metaphor of starlight is most helpful. When you look at a star in the night sky, a star radiates and shines its light for many millions of miles. A star does not try to shine; it does not work at it. Shining one's light is an effortless process. A star does not choose where it will shine its light. It simply radiates light.

As we radiate light effortlessly, as shamans and healers have done since the beginning of time, we have the power to transform illness, trauma, and environmental pollution. It is who we become that changes the world, not what we do. Obviously there are actions needed to live in harmony with the web of life. We need to change how we caretake the Earth. We need to wake up and live a shamanic way of life. And at the same time our natural, most basic presence can be a true healing force.

When in the presence of a great shaman, teacher, or spiritual healer, there is radiance emanating through her that also shines through her eyes. This presence heals everyone around her through a state of being rather than through the need to perform a healing technique. It is time for you to own your personal spiritual power so that *you* can be a healing presence of light.

Merging with a star will help you to understand how far your light will radiate and how effortless it is to be a light in the world. You just need to hold your intention and raise your consciousness to this desire.

JOURNEY TO MERGE WITH A STAR

Start with your preparation work so you can sink into the deep light within. Set your intention that you want to travel inward and merge with a star. You will learn about starlight by becoming starlight.

You are a walking star in the world. Experience how far your light shines and how it is not limited. Notice your potential to light up all around you and how effortless it is to shine and radiate. Notice how a star does not choose where to send its light. It simply shines. Experience yourself as starlight. You are a being of divine light, and you shine your light as brightly as the stars above you. This is your destiny.

Absorb this light into all your cells. When you feel ready to return, do not completely disengage from this starlight. Light is your true nature. Keep shining your light as you return to form, keeping that light flowing through you while managing it so that you can function in the world.

Once back from your journey take a short walk. Go out and engage in simple activities while in an illuminated state. This is a powerful and revealing way to see the world through the eyes of spirit. Notice how it feels to be lit from within. Notice if you feel different physically and if your attitude about life has changed.

In my workshops I play either "The Ultimate Om" by Jonathan Goldman, "Wavepool" by Robert Rand, or the bell and Tibetan bowl track on my music program *Soul Journeys: Music for Shamanic Journeys* to help participants hold a transfigured state. In my own personal practice I choose from a wealth of music created to heighten consciousness. You can experiment and find the music that works best for you.

Toning can also help you hold a transfigured state and prevent your egoic state of consciousness from distracting you. When you tone, you chant a vowel and hold it. Or you can chant the syllable *Om*.

AN ENDURING LUMINOUS STATE

Create a regular practice of transfiguration. Spend time bathing in your spiritual light and absorb the light into your cells. You want to learn how to hold a luminous state for longer periods of time throughout the day. It is not enough just to experience your spiritual light in the morning and then disconnect from your spiritual essence while you are out in the world. The key is to learn how to weave experiencing a spiritual state into your daily life. This takes time and practice as you want to stay grounded while you engage in your daily activities.

When I transfigure, I often experience my spiritual nature as the void, which is the place before light and form. Some of my students also report experiencing the void during their transfiguration practice. This is the same as experiencing the light of the divine except that you might experience blackness instead of the luminous light of a star. In experiencing the void when I transfigure, I still describe it as my divine light and feel myself as radiant as a star.

An issue I am frequently asked to address is how to transfigure during a wave of depression where you cannot experience your divine light. It is important to understand that your inner light is eternal. It never dims or goes out. But there are times when an emotional state might prevent you from being able to experience your inner starlight. During these times do whatever simple spiritual practices you have already been working with that remind you of the truth of who you are. Be with what is. Observe the state you are in. Ride the wave of your emotional state. In time you will move through the darkness into the light. Experiencing darkness is a fertile time where invisible growth is happening. When the time is right, you will burst forth into the light of life.

I have watched some wonderful transformations happen for people who practice transfiguration on a regular basis, including:

- veterans healing their PTSD
- people healing from a variety of emotional and physical illnesses
- people riding the waves of life in a more graceful fashion

> people staying grounded and centered while being
> witness and holding space for others who had become ill
> or suffered a catastrophic event

> people receiving chemotherapy feeling strong and healthy,
> relieved of the pain of their illness

> friends and students facing death transitioning from a
> state of grace and peace during their process of dying.

One night I had a dream where I was getting ready to perform a sacred ceremony to transfigure and radiate my light. I kept finding that I had to take off sweaters that were covering my spiritual nature. As I took off one sweater, I found there was another sweater to take off. The dream showed me how part of the practice is removing the layers of "clothing" that cover up our spiritual nature. And this is a work in progress.

The practice of transfiguration is a potent way to strengthen yourself. As you experience your divinity and perfection, you create a state within where your cells are once again connected and free to communicate with each other releasing the knowledge you were born with of how to heal. Think of a phone line that has been cleared, allowing your cells to communicate with each other again.

RADIATE YOUR LIGHT THROUGHOUT THE DAY

As you transfigure and experience a state of oneness instead of separation, you find calm in the midst of dense collective energies that often get lost in anger and fear. You can ride with grace both the smooth and turbulent waves in the river of life.

Start by setting aside time on a daily basis to experience yourself as divine light, starlight. Throughout the day radiate your light while you are waiting in line at the bank, grocery store, at the gas station, at work, walking, and engaging in all your daily activities. Be a light in the world. You are not sending light, and you are not healing others without being asked to. You are simply shining. Perceive others as beings of light.

Truly see the light of others shining as bright as the sun. It is not enough to mentally recognize that all of life is divine light. You must engage your full sensory awareness while seeing through the eyes of spirit and perceive the depth of others' light shining through. By doing so you truly uplift all of life. This is all part of your everyday empowerment of living a shamanic way of life.

HEALING WITH SPIRITUAL LIGHT

You have a tremendous amount of potential to be a positive change-maker in the world by adding the practice of transfiguration with how you perceive loved ones, friends, clients, and the world at large.

I have witnessed numerous changes where food, soil, and substances that were polluted were put in the middle of the circle during a transfiguration ceremony where all participants radiated their light. We tested the pH of water that had been polluted and after our ceremony observed how the pH returned toward neutral. A GDV (gas discharge visualization) camera has been used to photograph the energetic field of people, food, and substances before and after the ceremony. We put people and items such as cheddar cheese, crackers, fruit, artificial sweeteners, soil from a driveway, and even chocolate in the middle of the circle. Using the GDV camera, photos were also taken of people before and after they transfigured. In all the photographs we could see how the energy fields returned to a state of vitality after the ceremony. The results have been remarkable and inspiring![1]

I do believe that working with light will be how we heal in the future. In my practice I still perform soul retrievals, power animal retrievals, extraction of illness, and depossession work. Clients who come to see me still believe that this work is needed for their ultimate healing. But I also have evolved my work and bridge my transfiguration work into my shamanic healing practice. I also teach my clients how to experience their inner light and encourage them to create a regular meditation practice to soak in this light. This is one way to empower others in their process of healing.

Ben received a phone call from a childhood friend, who had just been diagnosed with breast cancer. Ben asked his friend if he could do some work on her behalf, and she agreed. Ben had been practicing healing with spiritual light with some of his clients with great success, and he proceeded to work in this way with his friend. Although his friend lived in another state, distance made no difference.

Ben transfigured daily and perceived his friend in her divine light. His friend started to notice an immediate difference in how she was feeling and also her attitude toward her diagnosis. She became interested in transfiguration, and Ben taught her the practice. The rapid improvement of her health surprised her doctor. She kept up the practice of transfiguration for herself and has no further health issues. Ben and his friend formed a deeper relationship and bond through the spiritual work they now practice together.

HOLDING THE PERSPECTIVE THAT HEALS

You always have the choice to see others as ill or suffering, or in divine light and perfection. In working with another person or with a world event, do not focus on the illness or catastrophe that has occurred. Do not energize the issue and complaint by focusing on it.

If a friend or client shares that she was given a terminal diagnosis of cancer by her doctors, don't focus on the illness. To do so feeds the power of the illness. This does not mean that you need to tell your friend or client that on a spiritual level her cancer does not exist. To say this is not therapeutic unless she is also trained to do a spiritual practice such as transfiguration. I have so many friends and students who are very cautious about who they share their medical diagnosis with. For with spiritual work if loved ones and friends move into a place of fear and start to project that onto another, this feeds the possibility of a negative outcome. Those dealing with serious medical conditions do not want to be pitied or have fear projected onto them. Many people do not want to carry the label of an illness.

In the ceremonies I lead we do not attempt to manipulate the environment. We do not focus on a problem with the people or substances in the middle of the circle, nor do we send healing energies to the people or substances. We change ourselves by transfiguring into divine light, perfection, and oneness with the understanding that our outer world will reflect back to us the inner changes that we make. This way of perception goes back to the ancient and spiritual principle of "as above, so below; as within, so without."

When working in this way, we perceive everyone and everything in its divine perfection. On a physical level there might be illness being reported. But on a spiritual level we recognize the divine perfection of all of life. In this way we do not feed the power of the illness; rather, we stimulate the radiance of each being to shine forth.

When my students send out e-mail requests for healing help, they word the request with, "Thank you for seeing me in my divine light." This is the ultimate state that we all want to feed. If someone is going into surgery, they add the request that the surgeon and all the medical staff responsible for their care are seen in their divine light also.

When I practice Healing with Spiritual Light when I work with clients, I listen with compassion to their presenting issue. In my own mind I use my invisible sight to perceive them in their perfect health. See all in its divine light and perfection. Then transfigure while focusing on the person and place and simply radiate your light. In this way you are not sending any energy or trying to heal someone or a community without permission.

Here is another wonderful example of the power of this work. It is a story that shows the benefit of being persistent and staying consistent and present.

Years ago Dory was contacted by the wife of a forty-two-year-old man who had had a stroke about five months prior to making contact with her.[2] The medical community had given up on his being able to progress any further, but his wife believed in his capacity to continue to improve. She had some familiarity with shamanism and asked if Dory would work with him. When Dory first met the man, he walked with the help of a cane, but was very slow and had significant balance issues. He had no feeling or ability to move his right arm, and he could not speak at all except to repeat the numbers "one" and "two." In the first three visits Dory performed classic shamanic healing methods on her client. There was really not much more she could do for him with traditional shamanic healing, and she shifted into working with the practice of transfiguration.

Dory began seeing her client once a week. She would sit next to him and transfigure while perceiving him in his divine light. She listened to meditative music that would help her spiritual expansion and also to help her hold a transfigured state. She held this state for about forty-five minutes to one hour each session. Dory encouraged her client to be present to the love and light of his true nature. He loved the work and beamed with joy at the end of the sessions. The light began to return to his eyes after about six meetings, and his increased cognition became evident. He did no other work during that year except some basic occupational therapy sessions. After about three months of weekly transfiguration sessions, he was able to walk without the cane and his balance was greatly improved.

About five months into their weekly sessions, Dory's client greeted her with a "Hello, Dory" when she opened the door. This created a lot of emotion for Dory, the client, and his wife. Slowly, his speech began to return, and within seven months of continuous weekly work, he was able to speak in full sentences. About eight months or so into the work together, he reported that he felt tingling in his right arm. Dory commented that maybe the nerves were beginning to regenerate and that he should focus on seeing his nerves reconnecting. The feeling began to return quite rapidly, and soon he was able to move his arm away from his body. At this point, Dory suggested he needed some physical exercise to rebuild the muscles. He began working with light weights and practiced holding objects in that hand.

By the time Dory and her client had worked together for nine months, he was able to cook dinner for his wife, make his own lunches, do laundry, mow the grass, go for walks, work on his stationary bike, go biking in the neighborhood, and communicate for short periods of time on the phone with friends and family. After about twelve months of weekly sessions, he was able to talk slowly but clearly and hold a conversation about many topics including golf, politics, his family, TV shows and movies, and books. He could read again. And he started to play golf again. He has a life in which he can talk, walk, write, and perform basic daily tasks. Although he has not been able to return to his work in the world, he is content and continues to seek new challenges.

This is just one example of the power of how shining light to stimulate a person's own inner radiance to heal from diagnoses that traditional medicine labels as untreatable. In a culture where we are so conditioned to be dynamic and take action, it is interesting to reflect on how bringing in the feminine aspect of *being* can have such a profound effect and impact on challenges we are facing personally and globally.

THE POWER OF UNCONDITIONAL LOVE

The greatest gift that we can share is to be a presence of light and also a vessel of unconditional love. Oftentimes people misinterpret the word *love,* for we typically use that word within our personal relationships. I am using the word *unconditional love* in the same way the creator loves creation.

I have had three near-death experiences. During one near-death experience, I traveled to a being I call God. God had no form or gender and just beamed light that held a vibration and frequency I had not witnessed before. I was standing in front of God, this radiant light being. What struck me was that God radiated love without seeing me as an individual personality and without judgment. God beamed love and light just as a star radiates without judging where that light goes.

I have had many lessons in life about the power of unconditional love, but I want to share one poignant story with you. My father died at the age of ninety-seven. I really adored my father. He was very good and loving toward me. He went through a difficult process when he was dying. His eyes were filled with terror, and it was really clear that he was re-experiencing traumas of his past. Due to his state of confusion, I could not have clear and rational conversations with him. But

I could be a pure vessel of light and love. I would sit with him, and it didn't matter what he was saying or what he did, I just held a state of love.

Because I took care of him, I was able to control who came into his presence. The only people who were allowed to assist in his care were people who could channel unconditional love. An incredible community of caregivers acting as a vessel of unconditional love surrounded my father. No matter what his behavior was, we held him in love. I watched as the terror in his eyes dissolved. I could see the healing that was taking place for him; during his final days he started beaming. Caregivers in his facility lined up to sit in his presence. My father died smiling and in a state of grace. It was obvious he worked through his past pain and had come to a place of peace. My experience with my father taught me a valuable lesson of how important it is to hold the collective in love.

You have gone through the process of disconnecting from the dense collective energies that do not support a state of spiritual health. You now might find that you desire to be a healing and compassionate presence in the world. As you witness how others behave and observe planetary challenges, you will have judgments. It is natural to judge the harmful behavior we witness toward others such as abuse, violence, and murder. But it is also important for you to do your spiritual work and learn how to hold the space as people heal from past traumas and wounds that led them to act violently toward others. For in this realm of human existence, we are all learning how to transform and let go of our past. Hold the space while traumas and violent behavior are being healed. Do your work to deal with your reactions and triggers. This does not mean you are approving of violence—rather you are transforming the world through the loving presence that you become. It is a great gift that you can share to beam light like a star in the night sky and be a vessel of unconditional love.

15

Listening *for* Guidance *beyond* Form, Time, *and* Space

I SEE MYSELF AS A SPIRITUAL EXPLORER. I do not profess to have all the answers to the great mysteries of the universe. I remember once commenting to my power animal that when I die, I will finally understand the mysteries of life. He responded to me, "What makes you think that?" I embrace and honor that I do not have complete understanding to all the answers to the mysteries of life. And I like the "not knowing" and surrendering to and living with the mystery.

At the same time I enjoy exploring the different dimensions in the hidden realms. There is an abundance of exploratory journeys into the invisible realms that you can take. In this chapter I share some journeys that I have led over the years in workshops that my students report benefiting from. May these journeys inspire your own explorations.

WORKING WITH THE FORMLESS ENERGY OF YOUR HELPING SPIRITS

I have described throughout *Walking in Light* that the helping spirits have no form. They appear to us as a form to meet the needs of our personality. The form they take often represents certain teachings that are important for us to embrace. During one workshop, while I was demonstrating to my group how to merge with a helping spirit, I merged with my teacher Isis. I told the group they could ask her questions.

Someone asked if Isis could see the power animals and teachers of all the participants in the circle. Isis's response was quite revealing. She responded by saying, "There are no power animals and teachers. You give them a form by giving them a name." After I disengaged from Isis, I reflected on what she said. The native people in Australia also share this teaching that when we name things, we give them a form. I thought about this teaching in regard to how we name our helping spirits. Once home from leading this workshop, I journeyed to Isis and asked her if I could merge with her expanded energy rather than in the form of a human. I had such a profound experience as I experienced a level of expansiveness that I had not felt before in a journey. The effects of this journey stayed with me for weeks. We limit the healing power of our helping spirits by projecting form onto them.

We limit healing because we experience ourselves in our human form. Then we merge with a helping spirit who we give a form to by naming it. And when working in behalf of a client, we perceive them as a form who is suffering. The perception of form limits the unlimited power available for healing. I have therefore shifted my work to inspiring my students to transfigure, to heal with spiritual light, and to merge with the formless energy of a helping spirit. And as I shared in chapter 14, it is important to let go of the labels of illness we impose on clients, loved ones, the public, other living beings, and the planet. Instead of seeing them challenged, perceive them in their divine light.

Your helping spirits will continue to present themselves in a form that provides comfort and teachings for you. Your helping spirits might remain your "best buddies." At the same time there will be situations where you can empower your practice by experiencing your helping spirit without form.

JOURNEY TO EXPERIENCE FORMLESS HELPING SPIRITS

Perform your preparation work and leave behind your ordinary thoughts and concerns. You can drum or rattle for yourself. Or you can listen to your favorite music for journeying.

Journey to meet up with a helping spirit that you have come to rely on for support and guidance. Ask your helping spirit to drop its form, allowing you to merge with its unlimited energy that has no boundaries.

Experience this immense power. You might ask for a healing from this formless being. You can also transfigure and then merge with the formless energy of your helping spirit. Notice any changes in your vibration and frequency as you do this. Depending on how much you have engaged in your spiritual practices, you might find you can only maintain this state for a few minutes. You might feel like the energy and vibration becomes more than you can physically handle. When you feel done, disengage from your helping spirit and return.

Before returning to the room you are journeying in, imagine yourself in a beautiful garden. Pick a tree you can sit with. As you sit with the tree, allow your energy to flow deep into the earth, rooting you back to the earth and in your body.

When you feel completely grounded, return.

Once you are back in your room, take some time to stretch and feel yourself fully present. You might have the afterglow and the experience of the power and light of your helping spirit shining through you. This is fine as you want to learn how to raise your frequency and become a stronger vessel of light throughout the day. If you feel like you have too much energy flowing through you, set your intention to disengage from any energies that you cannot physically handle at this time. Just by stating this intention, you will disengage from any energies that are too much for your nervous system.

Make sure that you add eating a healthy diet and an exercise routine into your life. You want to strengthen your body so you can handle bringing through higher spiritual vibrations.

Carol's mother was diagnosed with a heart problem. Carol asked her if she was open to some spiritual healing work. She was open to any help that she could get. Carol continued her transfiguration practice and perceived her mother in her divine light and perfect health. She added to her work by merging with the formless energy of her teacher and radiated light while focusing on the image of her mother. Carol's mom did heal, and this work deepened their relationship. She was eager to learn about experiencing her inner light, and now she has added this practice into her own healing regimen along with changing her lifestyle and diet.

A way to evolve your work is to acknowledge the unlimited power of your helping spirits when you perceive them as formless energies. And as you also perceive yourself as formless divine light, this adds exponentially to the outcome of whatever spiritual healing practice you engage in. You can be a vessel of this unlimited power when working for yourself, others, and the planet.

THE MULTIVERSE AND PARALLEL DIMENSIONS

There are people who believe in the multiverse and that there are parallel realities that exist along with the dimension of reality we live in. Wikipedia defines the multiverse as: "The hypothetical set of infinite or finite possible universes that together comprise everything that exists—the entirety of space, time, matter, and energy as well as the physical laws and constants that describe them." Multiverses have been hypothesized in cosmology, physics, astronomy, religion, philosophy, transpersonal psychology, and fiction. The various universes within the multiverse are called parallel universes. Parallel universes are also known as parallel dimensions.

For people who entertain the possibility that parallel universes and dimensions exist, it is believed that even though we are living in one reality right now, there are infinite lives that we are leading in parallel universes. Here is one example to describe this: Let's say in the past you were accepted to three different colleges. You had a strong desire to go to each of them, could not make up your mind, and were very challenged by the decision-making process. You made a choice in this reality, in the here and now, to go to one school. But in working with parallel realities, your world split, creating multiple realities where you also had lives in which you went to the other two schools. And in these three multiple realities, you lived different lives based on the choices you made. You met different friends, might have married different people in your different lives, and you ended up with different careers.

I have been very interested in multiple-reality theory for a long time, and I have shared some experiential exploratory journeywork with my students, for you can journey into different, multiple realities. I have met many students who were not aware of parallel universes but shared with me that they have traveled into other dimensions in a dream. As with any hypothesized theories, there are many nonbelievers in multiple and parallel realities. I am certainly not going to try and convince you of their existence. As shamanism is a practice of direct revelation, you can choose to journey and get information for yourself.

I teach journeying into parallel universes as a way to get knowledge about how you can evolve and improve the quality of your life. I do not advise using these journeys as a way to escape your present life and get caught up in living in another dimension. I do not support escapism. Get advice on how to live a happy and meaningful life in the here and now. The journeys can reveal valuable insights because in different realities, you can ask the version of yourself that inhabits that dimension what steps were taken that led to a successful, joyful, and meaningful life. You can follow the line of how different choices you face lead to different life experiences and the consequence of your choices.

Sarah was considering a move. She had applied for two different job positions that would lead her to changing her location from one state to another. Sarah ended up getting both jobs, and she had a difficult choice to make. Both locations attracted her, and she could not make a decision. Sarah was very experienced in shamanic journeying, so she knew she could consult with a helping spirit to ask for advice, but she also wanted to examine the life she would create based on her potential choices.

She journeyed and explored the life she would lead with her possible choices. Sarah was able to fully enter into the different lives that would be created from each choice. She could see who she would meet as well as where she seemed the happiest and successful. Once Sarah examined the lines of her life, she felt confident in making a decision that indeed led her to feeling like she was living a fulfilling life.

You can use this next journey to meet yourself in a parallel reality where you created the life you wish to live.

JOURNEY TO MEET YOURSELF IN A PARALLEL DIMENSION

Get ready for this journey by performing your preparation work. Set your intention that you would like to meet yourself in a parallel reality where you created the joy, success, and passion you wish to create for yourself now. Your intention will take you into the appropriate dimension. You can invite one of your helping spirits to travel with you and accompany you on this journey.

Once you meet yourself in the parallel dimension you are seeking, ask yourself questions. Ask for advice on steps that you can take that will lead you toward your desired outcome.

When you have received the advice you are seeking, return back to the room you are journeying in. Make sure you ground yourself back into present time. Imagine sitting with a powerful tree in nature and root yourself so that you feel grounded and fully present.

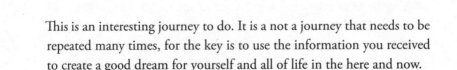

This is an interesting journey to do. It is a not a journey that needs to be repeated many times, for the key is to use the information you received to create a good dream for yourself and all of life in the here and now.

JOURNEYING BEYOND TIME

Whenever you perform a shamanic journey, you are journeying outside of time, for in the transcendent realms, time does not exist. There is no linear time. Therefore, when you journey, you can travel into another dimension of time and meet with ancestors or even historical and famous figures you would like to learn from. You can journey to native ancestral spirits who have teachings of how to return the planet to a state of health and well-being.

You can also journey into the future to learn from descendants. I love working in this way to learn about healing methods used in the future and how I can evolve my healing work.[1] I have built a very strong relationship with a group of descendants I have been journeying to for many years. I have had the honor of receiving powerful healings on me as they used advanced healing methods from the future. Descendants are very generous with the teachings they share with us, for their quality of life depends on the choices we make as their ancestors.

Joyce came to me asking for help. She was a professional violin player in an orchestra, and she was starting to have frequent panic attacks before each performance. She was passionate about playing her violin and did not want to leave the orchestra. But the panic attacks were creating too much stress and suffering for her. I performed some healing work for her and guided her on many of the exercises shared in *Walking in Light*. She also added journeying to a favorite historical violinist who taught her how she could prepare herself before a performance to maintain a state of peace and ease while she was playing.

Lola journeyed to meet a descendant to ask for guidance for how she could heal from an autoimmune disease she was suffering from. She had developed a strong transfiguration practice, but she wanted to see what else she could learn. Lola journeyed to a future time where she met a descendent who lived a very simple life in a forested area. In her time there were no more cities, and everyone lived a joyful and peaceful existence as they were connected with nature. The descendent was very impressed by how Lola could experience her spiritual light, and she guided Lola on how she could add using her voice to chant vowels and syllables that held a healing vibration.

You can also journey to yourself in the future and ask questions of your future self as you did with the last journey into a parallel dimension. Your future self will have a wealth of suggestions to share with you about changes you can make now that will improve your life in both the present and future.

Brian journeyed to his future self to ask for advice that would be helpful to him. He met with himself in his elder years. His future self encouraged him to spend more time doing activities that he loved to do instead of focusing all his attention on his career goals. He guided him in making better choices about the relationships he involved himself in, and also how to improve his attitude about life. This was good practice for Brian to engage in to reflect on the consequences of how he was living his life.

JOURNEY TO MEET YOUR FUTURE SELF

Set the intention that you wish to meet your future self who has worked with all the material presented in *Walking in Light* and successfully created a deep and meaningful life. Ask any questions of your future self about actions you need to take as well as changes you need to make to your current life that will assist in leading you toward your desired outcome. Your future self might help you to establish a healthy set of goals.

When you have received the guidance you are seeking, return back to the room you are in here and now, completely grounded and present. Take time to reflect on the answers you received and be inspired by observing the life you have ahead.

WORKING WITH THE ANCIENT ONES

The Anasazi Indians lived from AD 700–1200 in the Four Corners area of New Mexico, Colorado, Utah, and Arizona. The Anasazi were cliff dwellers as their homes were built into the walls of a cliff, and there are sites of cliff dwellings that can still be visited. The Anasazi disappeared simultaneously and mysteriously. Scientists have suggested a host of theories about what happened to the Anasazi. The theories only embrace rational, logistical, and scientific principles. They do not address the mystery of what happened to this group of people.

I have had the wonderful opportunity to visit a variety of Anasazi ruins. The first time I set foot in a national park of Anasazi cliff dwellings, I could hear the people laughing and talking. I could feel their presence, and I could smell the food as they were cooking it. My experience has been that the Anasazi are still here, but they shifted to a higher frequency and into another dimension of reality that we cannot see but still exists. Because I love exploring and learning about the wisdom of the ancients, I have led journeys in my workshops where as a group and loving community we visited the Anasazi to learn from them. They have shared a wealth of information about how to live a life filled with light and love that assists in shifting to living in a higher frequency.

Today there seems to be a wider gap in levels of consciousness. There are so many who continue to choose to live in a dense level of consciousness that embraces greed, inequality, power over, and separation. At the same time there are many making a shift and whose consciousness is evolving toward living a life filled with unconditional love and recognizing the light in all of life. This gap in the different levels of consciousness leads me to wonder if we will experience a split in dimensions at some point in time. Two parallel realities could be created as people continue to live in separate frequencies. This "theory" or wondering can seem very farfetched, but it is something I have been writing about and teaching for a number of years. I have found that visiting the Anasazi has helped me gain an understanding of how different dimensions can exist simultaneously.

There are other ancient civilizations that have lived an evolved existence. You might choose to do some exploratory journeys to meet with ancient advanced civilizations that you believe were highly evolved. For example, I have journeyed to the ancient Egyptians to learn how they really built their pyramids, statues, and temples. After visiting Egypt, the scientific explanation of how the Egyptians built their sacred sites did not make sense to me, for something beyond ordinary linear explanations seemed to have occurred. I received such an interesting response from one ancient Egyptian I met in a journey where

I asked how their sacred sites were built. I was told that I had no clue what the word *concentration* means. Think about it.

The ancestral spirits hold so many keys to the continuation of the planet, and their teachings need to be reintroduced and practiced today. The native people of the earth had practices and led ceremonies that contributed to the health of the community and the land. There is much knowledge and wisdom to be gained as we search for ways to be positive changemakers in the world we live in.

16

Sharing *the* Light

THERE IS A POWER that comes from working in anonymity. Often people confuse being in the role of a leader, healer, and changemaker with having to be public. A powerful model that embraces the feminine aspect of shamanism is being part of an invisible community that works together with concentration and the power of focused intent to shift the energy in the web of life.

THE INNER CHAMBER OF LIGHT

I had an enlightening journey on the power of working in anonymity. In my journey I was taken to a territory called the Inner Chamber of Light. Once there I was met by two faceless beings. The beings escorted me to what felt like my spiritual workstation. I could not see forms, but I was aware that there were many thousands of others who were doing spiritual work together in this Inner Chamber of Light. There was no talking, discussing philosophies, or comparing spiritual practices and teachings. Everyone just performed their work out of love for all of life. The power was tangible in this place. I was so touched as I embraced and felt the power of many thousands of people around the world doing their spiritual work in silence without having to be seen, recognized, and acknowledged for what they are doing. The power of focus, concentration, and working in unity is how we can gather as a global community to be a force of change and healing in the world today. It does not matter your education or what you do for work. We all can be a vessel of love and light.

In some of my workshops, we perform a ceremony where as a group we travel to the Inner Chamber of Light to find our personal spiritual workstation and also to experience the power of working anonymously. In this place you can feel on a cellular level the power of working in community with focused intent. I have shared this journey with the thousands of readers of my monthly column and have received such wonderful and positive feedback.

JOURNEY TO THE INNER CHAMBER OF LIGHT

Prepare yourself so you can enter into a deep spiritual state. Start by darkening the room you are in. Put something over your eyes. Even if you drum or rattle for yourself, tie a bandana or scarf over your eyes. I find that performing this journey in darkness adds to the power of being anonymous. Use music that heightens your consciousness. Set your intention to be led to the Inner Chamber of Light.

Once there you will be met by two faceless beings. They will not talk to you. They will simply lead you to your spiritual work-station; once there take a seat. Although words will not be spoken, you will sense and intuit instructions of what you should be doing to repair the web of life. You might find yourself sitting in silence while you work. You might get up and dance and move as you do the work as you have been guided. You might begin to tone, chant, or sing. As you do your work, sense the immense energy and connection with others working with focused intent. Know you are not alone in your work in behalf of life. Feel the hope and passion that guides your work.

Once you feel ready, send a telepathic message that you are ready to leave this chamber. The two guides who escorted you to your place will return to escort you back to the entrance of the

Inner Chamber of Light. Once at the entrance return back to the room you are in.

After returning, reflect on your experience. Take a walk in the fresh air with a sense of regained hope. As part of a community, your piece of work ripples and creates change throughout the web of life. Your unique gifts add to the entire world community.

CREATING A HUMAN WEB OF LIGHT

In the year 2000, I was inspired to create a global full moon ceremony. Since that time many thousands of people from around the world join me on the full moon in creating a human web of light that is woven within and throughout the Earth. Although this particular ceremony can be done daily, it is wonderful to join with others on a particular day. We join together in love on each full moon to weave a human web of love and light that embraces all of life.

I invite you to join in with this monthly ceremony. It is important to do some deep preparation before engaging in this ceremony, for so many of us only tap into the surface of the spiritual power available to us when we do not take the time to move into the appropriate state of consciousness. Before beginning, move out of an egoic state so that you are truly seeing through the eyes of spirit and fully experiencing your divine light. Expand your heart to be a vessel of unconditional love and create an inner state of harmony. Deepen your level of concentration, and stay focused on your vision no matter what the outcome. Remember that you are one with all of life and the creative force of the universe, and engage your imagination to dream the world that you want to live in into being. You are working within fertile ground as you experience your divine light and let it shine forth.

In the ancient tradition of alchemy, heavy-leaded consciousness was transmuted into golden light. In the Bible, Jesus challenges us not to hide our light under baskets. As I have shared, as mystics all over the world perform their miracles of healing, they are seen to shine and as luminescent. As you have experienced, you are light and you came here to shine. In this ceremony, Creating a Human Web of Light, experience your starlight and shine your light with others reflecting the beauty of the night sky.[1]

JOURNEY TO CREATE A HUMAN WEB OF LIGHT

Engage in this journey or meditation during the full moon. Again, preparation work is key to move you into a deep expanded state of consciousness.

Experience the love of your creator and absorb the love into your cells. Transfigure into your divine light. Feel the light radiating from the cells of your body with ease. In the spirit of unity, your light will begin to dance with the light of others.

Imagine your light connecting with the light of others all over the world. Join your light with others while holding the intention and using your imagination to experience yourself weaving a brilliant, sparkling web of light within and throughout the earth. Feel your heart pulse with love. Keep your focus, concentrate, and stay true to your intention. Allow your imagination to help you feel and see your internal light. Give yourself permission to let this light shine fully through you connecting to a radiant, vital, and translucent web. Let your light radiate and flow.

Once you have had the experience of weaving this web of light, either at the return beat or at your own time, begin your return. First absorb your light into all your cells. Open your eyes, feel your body, wiggle your toes, and return. Don't disconnect fully from your light. But disengage enough so that you can come back and function in your daily life.

You are part of a global community, and as we continue to feed this web of light, we bring this light to others and to the entire Earth. I invite you to continue to perform this journey on each full moon.

A COMMUNITY TO APPLY
THE POWER OF FOCUSED INTENT

As part of the evolution of your work, you might feel called to share some of the practices in *Walking in Light* with your friends and community. In the practice of shamanic healing it is well understood that there is an exponential power when we work in community versus when we work alone.

I have reflected quite a bit on the positive results that we saw in the Medicine for the Earth heart study that I conducted with the Integrative School of Medicine at the University of Michigan. The group was really devoted to the practices I taught, as I have shared in *Walking in Light*. We conducted follow-up phone calls with the group for six months after the workshop was completed. And the participants did keep up the practices and gained a state of hope from continuing the work. I continue to reflect on our time of being in circle together.

Some of the feedback participants shared during our time together was how they had never received so much love and support in a group. Tears would be shed as each participant shared their experiences of working together. There was so much support for each person. We prayed for the success and good health for each person. We not only focused on our own individual process, but we focused on the success of everyone in the group. After the workshop we continued to transfigure and radiate light to the group on a weekly basis. We kept this up during the six months of follow-up. Participants experienced for themselves how the love and support of the circle could create such powerful positive change in their lives. This touched the hearts of all who joined together in our circle. The group was so touched by and enthusiastic about working in community that we met one year later for a reunion. The participants were excited for all of us to meet each other's families and welcome them into our circle.

All the practices that I offer in *Walking in Light* can be shared with your friends and community. You work on a grander scale when you join with others to radiate light into the world. Here are some ways to share:

In challenging times you can teach people how to radiate love and light within the community and throughout the planet.

You can teach people the importance of radiating love and light and projecting strength onto others versus pitying others.

Share with others in your community the monthly full moon ceremony of weaving a human web of light.

Inspire people to transform the energy behind their thoughts so that they feed themselves and others with light.

Teach people in your community how to use words as blessings for others and for the world.

You can share how to reframe one's thoughts to lead to a positive outcome.

Share gratitude practices to help others shift their perception.

Show people how to integrate a practice of forgiveness into their lives to free themselves from the past.

Help people in your community to reconnect with nature and teach them the importance of honoring the elements that give us life.

Teaching others how to imagine and dream into being a world filled with harmony and peace is a gift you can give others in your community.

Create a prayer, wishing, or blessing tree in your community.

None of the practices you share with others need to involve the practice of shamanic journeying and working with helping spirits. These are all teachings about how to improve the quality of life. We can add to the power of what is being done in the ordinary realms with our spiritual work.

When we join our hearts together as a supportive community, we have great potential to transform what's happening on the planet. This does not mean that everybody in the community has to have the same religious or spiritual beliefs. We do not have to work in an identical way. We can create a world that embraces love, light, abundance, peace, and equality for all by working to create a beautiful field of mutual support. Together with each breath and each step that we take on this great Earth, we must live a life of honor and respect. We must join our hearts together as a global community and radiate love, weaving a beautiful web of light within and throughout this great Earth.

A TIME FOR REFLECTION AND CLOSING

When you started reading *Walking in Light* and engaging in the practices, you began a ceremony. You have been journeying on your own while at the same time joining together with the collective energies of others performing the same work. The ceremony you began as you started the work has come to completion. But the work needs to be continued.

In ancient times and in traditional cultures, the unseen and visible worlds were woven together. Today there is a solid doorway between the worlds. It is time for the veil to be lifted and to once again live a life of spirit with magic and beauty everywhere.

You have to do more than read books, take classes, perform journeys, and collect more information. It is important to find ways to evolve your life so that you are developing your inner life and are weaving spiritual practices into your daily life. As a collective we are being asked to live a life filled with spirit and walk the path of spirit.

THE DAILY LIFE OF A SHAMAN

Ceremony creates change. Live your life as a ceremony, and this will lead you to a process of positive change, following a path of spirit, and allowing you to ride a different wave in your life. This does not mean that you will not experience challenges and continued initiations. The challenges and initiations do create growth and evolution. All ceremonies have a beginning, middle, and end. When you started this work, you welcomed in your helping spirits and then you performed journeys and ceremonies that felt right for you to engage in. The journeys can be repeated again and again and will continue to deepen your spiritual growth. You ended each ceremony by giving thanks to the helping spirits and spiritual allies who participated in your process of healing and assisted you in gaining insights.

One of the questions asked by clients who have been given a "terminal" diagnosis is "Am I going to die?" The truth is that the process of healing leads to a death, for in order to heal from a serious illness, you have to die and create a new way of life. Death is not an end—it is a transition. Some people transition out of their body in order to heal. And sometimes the body heals but requires a transition to a new way of life. The strength of your inner spirit carries you through to the next stage of your healing. The practices you have and continue to do lead to a transition. You will not view your former life as the same anymore, and you have the best that life has to offer to look forward to.

Shamanism is a way of life. You must empower your life and bring these spiritual practices into your life and *live* them. There's a profound Haitian proverb that says, "The gods won't appear, the magic won't happen if you are not living your real life. Studying life is not living life and therefore has no magic." Here are the seeds I have offered you. It is up to you to nurture them and help them grow through intention, repetition, and application.

Continue to work with your helping spirits. Journey to the Lower, Middle, and Upper Worlds; your helping spirits will guide you. The helping spirits can see your life from a different perspective. Therefore, they have the power to act as wonderful guides as you continue your journey through life. Remember, you are a spirit too, and it is important to access your inner shaman.

Transmute the energy behind your thoughts and words. You are feeding yourself and the world with light. Remember, what you feed grows. What you give energy to, you give life to.

Dream the world you wish to live in into being. Use your words, thoughts, and imagination to create a life filled with meaning and passion. Dream a world filled with love, light, peace, harmony, equality, abundance, honor, and respect for all of life.

Stay connected to nature, to its cycles, and to the elements. Honor the elements each day, for they sustain you. Give thanks for all you receive from nature so that you may thrive. This will re-establish harmony within you. Whenever you experience harmony within, there will be harmony without in the world. This involves the spiritual principle of reciprocity. Allow yourself to be fully nourished by spending time in nature. Continue communicating with all of nature where you live and be attentive to the signs that guide your way.

Remember the truth of who you are. You are more than an ego; you *are* spirit; you *are* a being of divine light. You were created as a reflection of the creative forces of the universe. You were created from a place of unconditional love. Hold the vision of the world you wish to live in personally and collectively. Continue to surrender to spirit as you are guided to outcomes that are for your highest good and for the planet.

See the beauty in all things. Continue to live in a state of awe and wonder. Feel love and appreciation and remember to laugh at yourself. Follow your passion and always follow and believe in your creative inspiration. Remember your ancestors are working in your behalf. They love you, and they imparted gifts and strengths to you so you may thrive and be successful and healthy.

Continue to cultivate your inner garden. People in native cultures experience a richness and joy to life that is beyond what comes from focusing on the external world. They experience inner peace and happiness by cultivating a rich inner landscape. Make sure you are tending to your inner garden by traveling within and examining the conditions of the soil. Remove the seeds of defeatist and self-sabotaging thoughts and attitudes. Continue to plant the seeds of the words, thoughts, and dreams that lead to a positive outcome. Keep up your practices of gratitude and forgiveness as ways to grow beauty from your inner garden.

Do your preparation work. This will facilitate a strong state of concentration when you engage in spiritual work. Without concentration, you might not see the desired results. Learn how to let go of the distractions from life and fully engage in your spiritual work. It's important also to hold a strong focus and stay true to your intention while surrendering the outcome.

Always love yourself and keep moving forward. Don't forget in the darkness what you learned in the light. Stay focused, stay positive, and stay centered. Your love for life will always light your path through the smooth and turbulent times.

Continue to open. Let the wealth of ways that your helping spirits and spiritual allies show themselves to you. Change up your practices so they don't become too repetitive and routine. This is especially important when you engage in a ceremony that you repeat over time. You can easily lose the power of performing a ceremony that is repeated in a

routine fashion. Change how you prepare for your work.
And shift some of the ways you work so that your journeys
and ceremonies remain fresh.

I encourage you to continue with methods that allow you to enter
the unseen worlds and that assist you in returning easily to ordinary
reality. Keep focusing on grounding as you deepen your work. As you
continue, you will notice that your helping spirits dance more with
you in both worlds, as was done in ancient times.

As more people continue to embrace spiritual practices, the veils
between the worlds are becoming thinner. The spiritual work you do
does have power to create change. With your spiritual work, you weave
into reality an invisible world of substance that manifests physically in
the world. Feel the power of love. Continue to see from your heart
and your strong eye. This has always been the role of the shaman. And
remember, it is who you become that changes the world, not just what
you do. It is your birthright to shine as brightly as the stars above you.

Remember the community that you are part of. You gathered
to you an incredible community of helping spirits from the unseen
worlds. But you are also part of a wonderful community of people
around the world performing spiritual work in behalf of the web
of life. People are working in their own way, and that is beautiful.
The key is to work in collaboration and support of each other. Start
some of your blessings with statements such as, "We join our hearts
together on behalf of all of life." Include all spiritual practitioners
in the global community working together in your daily blessings
of gratitude. As we can work as a strong collective, we will dream a
new way of life into being that embraces love, light, harmony, peace,
equality, and abundance for all.

Continue to empower your daily life by living a shamanic way
of life.

Acknowledgments

I GIVE THANKS TO ALL the wonderful people at Sounds True I have gotten to know and work with. I am in deep gratitude to all the support Tami Simon has given me and my work over the years. And I thank Jennifer Holder for her brilliant visioning and editorial guidance. She was a true delight to work with. I am grateful for all the support I have received from Haven Iverson. I thank Mitchell Clute, who was the producer of my CD audio program *Shamanic Visioning,* from which this book was born.

I give thanks to my agent Barbara Moulton for her continual support and friendship. I am in deep gratitude to my husband Woods Shoemaker for all his love and continued support. I give gratitude to my students and readers of my *Transmutation News* who have trusted me to teach them how to create a shamanic way of life and also to work with divine light. Through their feedback I have learned so much about how to teach the practices to others. I give thanks to the teachers who I have trained for continuing to evolve their teachings of shamanism in such a brilliant way.

I give thanks to the helping spirits for the continual teachings of how to live a life filled with joy and meaning and the teachings of how to help others do the same. I am in deep gratitude to the Spirit of Santa Fe, the helping ancestors of the land, the Hidden Folk, the nature spirits, and the spirit of the arroyo where I live. During my walks I received such lovely guidance about additions to make to the material in the book.

I give thanks and honor my parents Aaron and Lee Ingerman. I could certainly feel my mom's presence while I was writing this book. I honor my ancestors, and I give thanks for my life.

Notes

PREFACE

1 For detailed information on how I worked with the group in the study, please read "Shamanic Intervention in a Cardiac Rehabilitation Program," pages 159–168 in *Spirited Medicine: Shamanism in Contemporary Healthcare,* edited by Cecile Carson, MD, with Tom Cowan, Bonnie Horrigan, and Jose Stevens.

2 Sara Warber, MD, et al., "Healing the Heart: A Randomized Pilot Study of A Spiritual Retreat for Depression and Acute Coronary Syndrome Patients," *Explore Journal,* 7, no. 4 (2011): 222–233.

INTRODUCTION

1 To read a full description on classic shamanic healing methods, you can read the articles I wrote titled *Abstract on Shamanism* and *Soul Retrieval* under Articles on www.sandraingerman.com.

CHAPTER 1

1 Sandra Ingerman and Hank Wesselman, *Awakening to the Spirit World* (Boulder, CO: Sounds True, 2010), 2.

CHAPTER 5

1 Simin Uysal, "Wishing Trees of Anatolia," http://anatolianstories. blogspot.com/2013/12/wishing-trees-of-anatolia.html.

CHAPTER 7

1 Imelda Almqvist is a gifted shamanic practitioner, teacher, and artist in the UK listed on shamanicteachers.com. She introduced me to the work of David Tacey. David Tacey, *Gods and Diseases: Making Sense of Our Physical and Mental Well-Being* (New York: Routledge, 2011), 162–163.

2 Tacey, *Gods and Diseases,* 162.

3 Tacey, *Gods and Diseases,* 163.

4 Ralph Metzner, *The Unfolding Self* (Novato, CA: Origin Press, 1986, 1988), 164.

5 Larry Peters, "Mystical Experience in Tamang Shamanism," *Trance, Initiation, and Psychotherapy in Nepalese Shamanism: Essays on Tamang and Tibetan Shamanism.* Revision, 13, no. 2 (1990): 79. This is really a wonderful essay about dismemberment that I highly recommend reading.

6 Edward Tick, *Warrior's Return: Restoring the Soul After War* (Boulder, CO: Sounds True, 2014).

CHAPTER 11

1 I designed an app titled *Transmutation* as a tool you can use to stop your negative and self-defeatist thoughts and attitudes and replace them with thoughts that lead to a positive outcome. This app has an alert that asks you to reflect on what you are thinking about throughout the day and a library filled with inspirational words, phrases, blessings, and photos.

CHAPTER 14

1 For information on the GDV camera and to view sample before and after photos of substances tested please visit shamanicteachers.com. Click on "Results." I also address this topic in further detail on pages 85–87 and 245–246 in *Awakening to the Spirit World,* co-written by Hank Wesselman (Boulder, CO: Sounds True, 2010).

2 Dory Cote is a brilliant shamanic practitioner and teacher in Maine who is listed on shamanicteachers.com.

CHAPTER 15

1 For more details on how I teach working with descendants read pages 176–177 of *Awakening to the Spirit World,* co-authored by Hank Wesselman, (Boulder, CO: Sounds True, 2010).

CHAPTER 16

1 For further instructions, visit sandraingerman.com and click on Creating A Human Web of Light. You can also use these instructions to share this work in your local community.

Further Reading

THERE IS A WEALTH of books that are now available on the practice of shamanism. The list is too vast to include all the wonderful books available. Here is a limited list for further reading. Also included are the books mentioned in *Walking in Light*.

Arrien, Angeles. *The Fourfold Way: Walking the Paths of the Warrior, Teacher, Healer, and Visionary*. New York: Harper Collins, 1993.

Carson, Cecile. *Spirited Medicine: Shamanism in Contemporary Healthcare*. Baltimore: Otter Bay Books, 2013.

Cowan, Eliot. *Plant Spirit Medicine: The Healing Power of Plants*. Columbus, NC: Granite Publishing, 1991.

Cowan, Tom. *Fire in the Head: Shamanism and the Celtic Spirit*. San Francisco: HarperOne, 1993.

Cowan, Tom. *Shamanism as a Spiritual Practice for Daily Life*. Berkeley, CA: Crossing Press, 1996.

Cowan, Tom. *Yearning for the Wind: Celtic Reflections on Soul and Nature*. Novato, CA: New World Library, 2003.

Deatsman, Colleen. *The Hollow Bone: A Field Guide to Shamanism*. San Francisco: Weiser Books, 2011.

Eliade, Mircea. *Shamanism: Archaic Techniques of Ecstasy*. Princeton: Princeton University Press, 1964.

Harner, Michael. *Cave and Cosmos: Shamanic Encounters with Another Reality*. Berkeley, CA: North Atlantic Books, 2013.

Harner, Michael. *The Way of the Shaman: A Guide to Power and Healing*. New York: Harper Collins, 1980.

Hart, Sparrow. *Letters to the River: A Guide to a Dream Worth Living*. Seattle: CreateSpace Independent Publishing Platform, 2013.

Ingerman, Sandra. *A Fall to Grace*. Vancouver, BC: Moon Tree Rising Productions, 1997.

Ingerman, Sandra. *How to Heal Toxic Thoughts: Simple Tools for Personal Transformation*. New York: Sterling, 2007.

Ingerman, Sandra. *Medicine for the Earth: How to Transform Personal and Environmental Toxins*. New York: Three Rivers Press, 2001.

Ingerman, Sandra. *Shamanic Journeying: A Beginner's Guide*. Boulder, CO: Sounds True, 2006.

Ingerman, Sandra. *The Shaman's Toolkit: Ancient Tools for Shaping the Life and World You Want to Live In*. San Francisco: Weiser Books, 2010.

Ingerman, Sandra. *Soul Retrieval: Mending the Fragmented Self*, rev. and updated ed. San Francisco: HarperOne, 2011.

Ingerman, Sandra. *Welcome Home: Following Your Soul's Journey Home*. San Francisco: HarperOne, 1993.

Ingerman, Sandra, and Llyn Robers. *Speaking with Nature: Awakening to the Dream of the Earth*. Rochester, VT: Inner Traditions, 2015.

Ingerman, Sandra, and Hank Wesselman. *Awakening to the Spirit World: The Shamanic Path of Direct Revelation*. Boulder, CO: Sounds True, 2010.

Mehl-Madrona, Lewis. *Coyote Medicine: Lessons from Native American Healing*. New York: Touchstone, 1998.

Mehl-Madrona, Lewis. *Healing the Mind through the Power of Story: The Promise of Narrative Psychiatry*. Rochester, VT: Bear & Company, 2010.

Metzner, Ralph. *The Ecology of Consciousness* (Vols 1–7), Berkeley, CA: Green Earth Foundation & Regent Press, 2005–2013.

Metzner, Ralph. *The Unfolding Self: Varieties of Transformative Experience*. Novato, CA: Origin Press, 1998.

Montgomery, Pam. *Plant Healing: A Guide to Working with Plant Consciousness*. Rochester, VT: Bear & Company, 2008.

Moss, Nan, and David Corbin. *Weather Shamanism: Harmonizing Our Connection with the Elements*. Rochester, VT: Bear & Company, 2008.

Moss, Robert. *Dreaming the Soul Back Home: Shamanic Dreaming for Healing and Becoming Whole.* Novato, CA: New World Library, 2012.

Narby, Jeremy. *The Cosmic Serpent: DNA and Origins of Knowledge.* New York: Tarcher, 1998.

Narby, Jeremy. *Intelligence in Nature: An Inquiry into Knowledge.* New York: Tarcher, 2006.

Perkins, John. *Shapeshifting: Shamanic Techniques for Global and Personal Transformation.* Rochester, VT: Destiny Books, 1997.

Poncelet, Claude. *The Shaman Within: A Physicists Guide to the Deeper Dimension of Your Life, the Universe, and Everything.* Boulder, CO: Sounds True, 2014.

Roberts, Llyn. *Shapeshifting into Higher Consciousness: Heal and Transform Yourself and Our World with Ancient and Modern Day Methods.* Abingdon, Oxon, UK: O Books, 2011.

Rysdyk, Evelyn. *A Spirit Walker's Guide to Shamanic Tools: How to Make Drums, Masks, Rattles, and Other Sacred Implements.* San Francisco: Weiser Books, 2014.

Rysdyk, Evelyn. *Spirit Walking: A Course in Shamanic Power.* San Francisco: Weiser Books, 2013.

Some, Malidoma Patrice. *Of Water and Spirit: Ritual, Magic, and Initiation in the Life of an African Shaman.* New York: Penguin, 1994.

Star Wolf, Linda, and Anna Cariad Barrett. *Sacred Medicine of Bee, Butterfly, Earthworm, and Spider.* Rochester, VT: Bear & Company, 2013.

Stevens, Jose. *Awaken the Inner Shaman: A Guide to the Power Path of the Heart.* Boulder, CO: Sounds True, 2014.

Sulis, Janet Elizabeth. *The Rush Hour Shaman: The Shamanic Practices for Urban Living.* Blue Ridge Summit, PA: Moon Books, 2014.

Tacey, David. *Gods and Diseases: Making Sense of Our Physical and Mental Wellbeing.* New York: Routledge, 2013.

Tick, Edward. *Warrior's Return: Restoring the Soul After War.* Boulder, CO: Sounds True, 2014

Villoldo, Alberto. *Mending the Past and Healing the Future with Soul Retrieval.* Carlsbad, CA: Hay House, 2006.

Villoldo, Alberto. *Shaman, Healer, Sage: How to Heal Yourself and Others with Energy Medicine of the Americas.* New York: Harmony, 2000.

Wesselman, Hank. *The Bowl of Light: Ancestral Wisdom from a Hawaiian Shaman.* Boulder, CO: Sounds True, 2011.

Wesselman, Hank. *The Journey to the Sacred Garden: A Guide to Traveling in the Spiritual Realities.* Carlsbad, CA: Hay House, 2003.

Wesselman, Hank, and Jill Kuykendall. *Spirit Medicine: Healing in the Sacred Realms.* Carlsbad, CA: Hay House, 2004.

Resources

A POWERFUL WAY TO ENGAGE in shamanic journeywork is to work in a group. You can begin your own local group sharing what you have learned in *Walking in Light*. The group can read and practice the exercises together.

Shamanicteachers.com is designed to help you find workshops on shamanic journeying, healing, planetary healing, and how to live a shamanic way of life. The site also lists hundreds of shamanic practitioners from around the world. This is an international alliance of dedicated shamanic practitioners and teachers trained by Sandra Ingerman who join together in the spirit of love, cooperation, and collaboration to share shamanic practices.

Sandra writes a monthly column in which she inspires the spiritual global community to keep working with spiritual practices even if we do not see immediate results from the work we are doing. The monthly column is titled Transmutation News. We also engage in the full moon ceremony Creating A Human Web of Light. Volunteers translate the column into many languages. The column can be read by visiting sandraingerman.com. Click on Transmutation News.

On sandraingerman.com you can also read articles on shamanic journeying and healing and the Medicine for the Earth work written by Sandra by clicking on Articles. You can also listen to a wealth of interviews by clicking on Interviews.

For more in depth instructions in the practice of shamanic journeying please read *Shamanic Journeying: A Beginner's Guide* and *Awakening to the Spirit World: The Shamanic Path of Direct Revelation* (co-written with Hank Wesselman).

Music for shamanic journeying, such as *Soul Journeys: Music for Shamanic Practice* and *Music for Shamanic Visioning: Taiko Drumming Journeys,* can be found by visiting Sounds True, soundstrue.com, or you can order from sandraingerman.com by clicking on Books and CDs. Also available is a program of guided journeys, *Shamanic Meditations: Guided Journeys for Insight, Vision, and Healing.*

Visit the app store on your mobile device to purchase the app Sandra created titled *Transmutation.* The app helps you to shift your negative thoughts to those that lead to your desired outcome. You can set an alert that asks you to reflect on what you are thinking about throughout the day and inspires you to shift your thoughts by viewing words, phrases, blessings, and photos that are provided in the Library.

If you are interested in ordering *The Ultimate Om* by Jonathan Goldman, visit healingsounds.com.

To order *Wavepool* by Robert Rand, visit robertwrand.com.

Index

About the Author

Sandra Ingerman, MA, is the author of ten books, presenter of seven audio programs, and creator of the *Transmutation* app. She has been teaching for more than thirty years. She teaches workshops internationally on shamanic journeying, healing, and reversing environmental pollution using spiritual methods. She has trained and founded an international alliance of Medicine for the Earth Teachers and shamanic teachers. Sandra is recognized for bridging ancient cross-cultural healing methods into our modern culture addressing the needs of our times.

Sandra is devoted to teaching people how we can work together as a global community to bring about positive change for the planet. She is passionate about helping people to reconnect with nature and remember that the Earth is our home.

Sandra is a licensed marriage and family therapist and professional mental health counselor. She is also a board-certified expert on traumatic stress as well as certified in acute traumatic stress management. She was awarded the 2007 Peace Award from the Global Foundation for Integrative Medicine. Sandra was chosen as one of the Top Ten Spiritual Leaders of 2013 by *Spirituality and Health* magazine.

About Sounds True

SOUNDS TRUE is a multimedia publisher whose mission is to inspire and support personal transformation and spiritual awakening. Founded in 1985 and located in Boulder, Colorado, we work with many of the leading spiritual teachers, thinkers, healers, and visionary artists of our time. We strive with every title to preserve the essential "living wisdom" of the author or artist. It is our goal to create products that not only provide information to a reader or listener, but that also embody the quality of a wisdom transmission.

For those seeking genuine transformation, Sounds True is your trusted partner. At SoundsTrue.com you will find a wealth of free resources to support your journey, including exclusive weekly audio interviews, free downloads, interactive learning tools, and other special savings on all our titles.

To learn more, please visit SoundsTrue.com/freegifts or call us toll free at 800-333-9185.

SOUNDS TRUE
many voices, one journey